D0729416

CONTENTS

MICHAEL BOOTH

Journalist and travel writer Michael Booth was dragged to live in Copenhagen six years ago – much as the Vikings had done to the English a millennium before – by his wife, who was born there. Much to his surprise, he discovered he rather liked it and, as the years passed and his glottal-swallowing Danish accent improved, he realised that the Danes weren't shouting at him all the time – that's just how they spoke. Since then he has grown to love the people's humour, culture, open-mindedness and myriad ways with a herring, and their capital city, which is compact, pretty, dynamic and, like their herring, deeply rewarding once you get to know it. Michael has written a book, *Just As Well I'm Leaving*, about his experiences in Denmark and his obsession with their national literary hero, Hans Christian Andersen. He has also written for all of the UK broadsheet newspapers and writes for the Sunday edition of the *Independent*, among other publications at home and abroad. He has just finished a memoir of a year spent in Paris learning to be a chef, *Sacré Cordon Bleu* (Cape), to be published in early 2008.

THE PHOTOGRAPHER

Raised in the Scottish Highlands, Jonathan Smith graduated from St Andrews University in 1994 with an MA in German. Unsure of what to do with his life, he took a flight to Vilnius and spent the next four years travelling around the former USSR. Having tried everything from language teaching to translating Lithuanian cookery books into English, Jon resolved to seek his fortune as a freelance travel photographer. Since then Jon's byline has appeared in over 50 Lonely Planet titles.

Cover photograph Bicycles parked in Kongens Nytorv, Michael Juno/Photolibrary. **Internal photographs** p36-37 Brian Harris/Axiom; p26, p102, p155 Cees van Roeden/Wonderful Copenhagen (WoCo); p24, p28, p29, p30, p67, p77, p153 Christian Alsing/(WoCo); p137 Gunter Lenz/Nordicphotos/Alamy; p23 Ireneusz Cyranek/(WoCo); p14 Keld Navntoft/AFP/Getty Images; p20 Louise Wilson/Getty Images; p162 Magnus Ragnvid/(WoCo); p151, p157 Morten Bjarnhof/(WoCo); p95 Radisson SAS Royal/(WoCo); p92 Tivoli/(WoCo); p149 The Square/(WoCo); p27, p101, p111, p148 (WoCo). All other photographs by Lonely Planet Images, and by Jonathan Smith except p140 Anders Blomqvist; p55 Holger Leue; p124, p150 Martin Llado; p122 Martin Moos .

THIS IS COPENHAGEN

You'd be mistaken in thinking the Danish capital had been designed specifically for the short-break traveller. It's a compact, comprehensive city, but it still manages to cram a millennium of history and culture within its historic heart.

Copenhagen is the most cosmopolitan and accessible of all the Scandinavian capitals. This urban oasis of calm, culture and conviviality is packed with some excellent museums, art galleries and unique monuments, as well as plenty of enchanting, historic streets and other beguiling urban areas that are perfect simply for a stroll and a gawp. The same attributes that are said to give its inhabitants one of the finest qualities of life in the world – its cleanliness, efficiency, safety and a superb infrastructure – work very much in the visitor's favour as well.

The city is remarkably compact and user-friendly. You can walk across it in a morning, or scoot about on the excellent metro and buses in minutes. Or you can just as easily spend an hour browsing in areas such as Ravnsborggade or Elmegade, or an afternoon getting to know the locals – fluent in English, course – in a cosy café.

Where Copenhagen really excels is in its marriage of old and new. Gabled 17th-century town houses, cobbled squares, canals and green-copper spires may define the aesthetic of this royal city but radical architecture, new trends and technologies and, of course, that famously discerning design sense are equally in evidence. Copenhagen has largely resisted the tyranny of the chain store so its independent shops – interior design and fashion are major strengths – are a big part of its appeal.

And if you are looking for a fairy-tale experience, nobody does it better than the Danes. Hans Christian Andersen lived in Copenhagen for most of his life, and the architecture and atmosphere that inspired him are waiting to charm, excite and delight you too.

Top left Café culture on Sankt Hans Torv, Nørrebro (p70) **Top right** Antique shopping in Nørrebro (p67) **Bottom** The lion statue at Det Kongelige Bibliotek (p101) looks up at the modern Black Diamond extension, Slotsholmen

Greenland exhibition at the Nationalmuseet (p16)

HIGHLIGHTS

> 1 TIVOLI GARDENS

UNLEASH YOUR INNER CHILD AT TIVOLI GARDENS, DENMARK'S PERENNIALLY POPULAR TOURIST DRAW

Denmark's number one tourist destination offers a beguiling blend of flower park, fun park, beer garden and food pavillions located slap-bang in the city centre. It is, in other words, as far removed from Disney as you can get. Depending on your mood, Tivoli will either enchant with its fanciful architecture, theatres and concert halls, boating lakes, world-famous lighting displays, fireworks and – these days – actually quite exciting rides (the Demon rollercoaster is brief but terrifying), or overpower you with its sugary schmaltz. Everything, from the entry fee to the cost of rides (not included in the entry fee) to the food on offer here is expensive. A good tip is to go on Fridays when, during summer, live bands play on the open-air stage. You can sometimes catch major international music acts (Sting, Brian Wilson, Tony Bennett) playing for free here; come early to secure a good vantage point. Every Wednesday and Friday Tivoli ends the day with a fireworks display at 11.45pm. See also p92.

>2 RUNDETÅRN

CLIMB THE SPIRE OF THE REMARKABLE RUNDETÅRN FOR A VIEW OVER THE MEDIEVAL HEART OF THE CITY

Haul yourself to the top of the 34.8m-high, red-brick 'Round Tower' and you will be following in the footsteps of such luminaries as King Christian IV, Denmark's famous Renaissance king who built it in 1642, and the hoofsteps of Tsar Peter the Great's horse, all the way up the tower's unique cobbled, spiral ramp to the open-air platform at the top. (Legend has it, someone even drove a car up there in 1902.) From here you'll find the city view has hardly changed since Peter's journey in 1716 and it is the perfect place to get your bearings.

Christian built the Rundetårn, which is attached to Trinitatiskirke (Trinity Church), as an observatory for the famous astronomer Tycho Brahe and it still functions as an excellent stargazing platform (it is the oldest functioning observatory in Europe and is open to the public from October to March). On the outside wall is a commemorative shield and the letters RFP, which stand for Christian's motto, translated as 'Piety Strengthens the Realm'. Halfway up the tower is an exhibition space with regularly changing displays of art and architecture. See also p110.

>3 CHRISTIANIA

LET YOUR HAIR DOWN IN THE ALTERNATIVE COMMUNITY OF CHRISTIANIA

Its counterculture glory days are long gone and the modern world is threatening its very survival, but Christiania, the infamous 'alternative community', remains one of Copenhagen's most distinctive and memorable experiences. It is home to a diverse bunch of highly principled counterculture pioneers, craftspeople, environmentalists, old-fashioned hippies and, it has to be said, alcoholics and junkies.

Back in 1971, when the community was founded by militant squatters who broke into a group of disused naval barracks in the heart of Christiania, they would probably have been labelled 'drop-outs' or part of 'the underground'. These days many of their once-radical ideas about recycling, organic food, free love and drug enlightenment have been adopted by the mainstream so, you might wonder, what's the point of Christiania today? Certainly many in Copenhagen have been pushing for its abolition and the developers have been eyeing this piece of land in the well-to-do canal quarter of Christianshavn for years.

At the time of going to print the government has offered the governing council of Christiania the chance to agree to a programme of 'normalisation' of the camp, which will involve it returning to government control but with the Christianites still having some say over its running. The Christianites have yet to agree and are continuing to dig their heels in but the prevailing view in Copenhagen is that change is going to happen with or without their consent.

For now, however, Christiania still has a unique atmosphere – part shambolic circus, part makeshift architectural expo, part hippy commune. Once past the squalid main drag, Pusher Street, with its roaming dogs and intimidating drunks, you will find yourself amid crumbling 18th-century barracks and an oddball array of makeshift housing, from converted railway carriages to pyramids, many with attractive waterside views of the old city ramparts. Christiania has several cafés, restaurants, shops and live-music venues, each of which usually has something distinctive on offer. See it while you still can. For more on Christiania and the surrounding area, see p42.

>4 LOUISIANA

TAKE A TRAIN BESIDE THE SEA TO THE MAJESTIC MODERN ART MUSEUM, LOUISIANA

One of the finest collections of international contemporary art in Scandinavia is housed in what is also one of the region's most beautiful museums. Louisiana (named after the founder's wife) is situated beside the waters of the Øresund sea, amid dappled woodland on grassy knolls with views across the water to Sweden. It is an exceptional setting but Louisiana has a collection to match its surroundings (thought not always as tranquil), including a number of pieces from the CoBrA movement (the name stands for 'Copenhagen, Brussels and Amsterdam', the home cities of its members). Notable works are by the leading member, Danish artist Asger Jørn, as well as international names such as Bacon, Warhol, Lichtenstein, Oldenburg, Rauschenburg, Rothko and Picasso. The museum has a very strong sculpture collection – many pieces are on view in the gardens – including works by Miro, Calder, Moore and Max Ernst. There is an entire room dedicated to Giacometti and a number of notable German artworks from the 1970s. Louisiana makes for an excellent afternoon trip; kids, who are well catered for here, love it too. Bring a picnic or enjoy the al fresco food at the museum's own excellent café-restaurant with its homemade cakes and Italian sandwiches. A changing programme of temporary exhibitions showcasing major artists draws massive crowds. See also p66.

>5 ROSENBORG SLOT

GOGGLE AT THE CROWN JEWELS AND OTHER TREASURES OF ROSENBORG SLOT

One look at the turreted, moated Rosenborg Slot (*slot* can refer to either a castle or a palace) and you might even believe fairytales can come true. This picturesque early-17th-century castle started out as a royal summer house situated, at that time, well beyond the city walls and grew over the years into this magnificent Renaissance palace. It's now home to part of the stunning royal collection of art, furniture and, in the basement, the crown jewels. Christian IV, Denmark's 'Sun King', began the building's transformation in 1606 and the palace was used as a royal summer residence until Frederik IV built Fredensborg Slot (p75), in mid-Zealand, in the early 18th century. Today the palace's 24 upper rooms, each as it was when their respective kings lived there, contain furnishings and portraits spanning 300 years of the Danish royal family up to the 19th century, but perhaps the main attraction lies in the basement. This is where you will find the crown jewels, including Christian IV's ornate crown, the jewel-studded sword of Christian III and many of the current queen's diamonds and emeralds. The palace overlooks Kongens Have (the King's Garden), an elegant formal park popular with sunbathers and families. For opening hours, see p82.

>6 NATIONALMUSEET

LEARN THE TRUTH ABOUT THE VIKINGS AT NATIONALMUSEET (THE NATIONAL MUSEUM)

The Danes are fiercely proud of their history and rightly so. There have been times when over half of northern Europe was ruled by Denmark, including most of Scandinavia, Iceland, some of northern Germany and even parts of eastern and southern England. The empire was founded by the Vikings – not nearly as rampaging and brutal as history has made them out to be. That said, they could rape and pillage with the best of them and continued doing so well into the 17th century. This excellent, modern museum covers all of that and more with particularly strong Viking and Renaissance collections, Stone Age finds, rune stones and staggering Bronze Age finds (not least the *lurene*, or horns, some of which date back over 3000 years ago and can still produce a note), as well as ancient Egyptian, Roman and Greek artefacts. The coin collection is housed in an especially beautiful room overlooking Christiansborg Slot. There is a superb children's museum on the ground floor packed with castles and costumes, plus a café and shop, while the top floor houses a charming toy museum. What's more, entrance is free. See also p90.

>7 SMØRREBRØD

ENJOY A CLASSIC DANISH OPEN SANDWICH AT IDA DAVIDSEN

Sushi and sandwiches have changed the way Danes snack just as they have everywhere else in the Western world, but they still hold a place in their heart for the traditional lunchtime Danish open sandwich, or smørrebrød. There are small takeaway smørrebød restaurants dotted throughout the city each displaying their not always appetising wares in the window (cold boiled eggs with remoulade and beetroot, anyone?).

The doyen of the genre is Ida Davidsen, whose small, unostentatious *kælder* (cellar) restaurant in the royal quarter of Frederiksstaden is renowned throughout the land. Here you can sample 177 different sandwich toppings, ranging from your everyday boiled potatoes and herring to rather more refined fare, such as smoked salmon, dill mayonnaise, caviar and crayfish (that one's named after the late Danish comic, Victor Borge). Ida, who still works here every day, is of the fifth Davidsen generation to work here. Her sons are carrying on the tradition, working alongside her behind the counter. See also p59.

>8 NØRREBRO

EXPLORE THE COOL SHOPS AND VIBRANT NIGHTLIFE IN NØRREBRO

These days two city quarters vie for the title of hippest place in Copenhagen: Vesterbro (p128) and Nørrebro (p64). Though Vesterbro has its share of great shops and bars – not to mention the ultimate club complex, Vega (p136) – we reckon Nørrebro just shades it in the hip stakes.

Though it isn't very big, you could spend an enjoyable day wandering within the boundaries of this densely packed, ethnically diverse residential, shopping and nightlife area which stretches from the elegant, shallow lakes (built in the 18th century as a fire break) to the north of the city centre. Nørrebro means 'north bridge', after the bridge that spans the lakes and which bears the main shopping street that rumbles through the heart of the district. It passes the historic Assistans Kirkegard (the cemetery that is home to so many Danish artists, writers, thinkers and politicians) and continues to the suburbs beyond. On either side lie fascinating streets such as Blågardsgade, with its delis and street cafés; Ravnsborggade, lined with bric-a-brac and antique shops and yet more cafés and restaurants; and trendy Elmegade, with its bars, cafés and streetwear stores. Nørrebro's pulsing heart lies in Sankt Hans Torv (Saint Hans' Square), with its cafés, ice-cream parlours and, just around the corner, the club Rust (one of the city's best; see p77) and the excellent independent Empire Cinema complex.

>9 DANISH DESIGN

REDESIGN YOUR LIFE, DANISH STYLE

Is there a more design-conscious nation than Denmark, or a more design-obsessed capital than Copenhagen? Sure, the Italians like a nice sofa and the French have their frocks, but in Denmark design excellence runs deeper than that. The Danes can't lift a fork to their mouth without first determining the designer and scoring the cutlery out of ten for function and form. Visit a Danish home and you will invariably find a Bang & Olufsen stereo in the living room, Poul Henningsen lamps hanging from the ceiling, Arne Jacobsen chairs (or at least copies) in the dining room, and Bodum glassware in the kitchen. This national obsession is celebrated at the Dansk Design Center just across from Tivoli on HC Andersens Boulevard. And to prove the Danes are no chauvinists, the Center usually fills its ground-floor exhibition space with the work of international designers, keeping its Danish classics on permanent display in the basement. See also p90.

>10 THE ROSKILDE & JAZZ FESTIVALS

CELEBRATE THE BEST IN MUSIC, FROM SMOOTH JAZZ TO INDIE POP, AT COPENHAGEN'S HOTTEST FESTIVALS

Thanks to one of those all-too-rare confluences of scheduling for travellers, two of Europe's most celebrated and enjoyable music festivals take place in and close to Copenhagen in early July each year.

The Roskilde Festival is mainland Europe's largest rock festival, drawing crowds of 80,000. It takes place in fields a 15-minute walk from Roskilde city centre and is renowned for its relaxed, friendly atmosphere. Some of the world's hottest rock and pop acts perform here on several outdoor stages – to give you some idea, the 2007 festival boasted a line-up that included The Who, Red Hot Chili Peppers and My Chemical Romance. That said, the festival is as much about the smaller, more marginal acts as the big names and it is, of course, especially good at identifying new music trends in Scandinavia.

The first festival was held in 1971 and drew a crowd of 10,000. Today over 150 rock, techno, trance, world-music and jazz acts play

here; recent years have even seen some classical performances. You can buy tents for 500kr to 1000kr on arrival and there is a vast camping place which, as always at these kind of things, offers the barest of facilities. Come on the Wednesday before the main weekend to nab the best places. For more details, see p156.

Meanwhile, in Copenhagen the city's Jazz Festival is the biggest entertainment event of the Copenhagen year, with 10 days of music beginning on the first Friday in July. It energises the city like nothing else, bringing not just live music to its streets, canal-sides and an eclectic mix of venues, but creating a tangible buzz of excitement in the air. There are usually over 1000 different concerts held in every available space – in fact, the city itself becomes a venue. The first Festival took place in 1978. Since that time it has mushroomed into one of Europe's leading jazz events. Over the years, performers have included such renowned names as Dizzy Gillespie, Miles Davis, Sonny Rollins, Oscar Peterson, Ray Charles and Wynton Marsalis. Tony Bennett, Herbie Hancock and Keith Jarrett are regulars, as are Denmark's own Cecilie Norby and David Sanborn. The festival programme is usually published in May.

For a selection of the best jazz venues in the city, see p157.

>11 STATENS MUSEUM FOR KUNST

MARVEL AT THE EXCEPTIONAL ART COLLECTION AT STATENS MUSEUM FOR KUNST (THE NATIONAL GALLERY)

The National Gallery of Denmark is divided into two main sections. The original, late-19th-century building houses six centuries of European art ranging from medieval works with stylised religious themes, through to the Renaissance, with impressive collections of Dutch and Flemish artists including Rubens, Breughel, Dürer and Frans Hals. As you would expect, the museum also has the best collection of Danish 19th-century art in the world, featuring leading artists from the Golden Age, such as Eckersburg, Købke, Krøyer, JT Lundbye, Vilhelm Hammershøi, LA Ring and Michael Ancher. Meanwhile, over in the spectacular glass-and-concrete modern extension by architect Anna Mario Indrio, you'll find more contemporary Danish artists, such as Per Kirkeby, Richard Mortensen and Asger Jørn, as well as foreign artists ranging from Matisse (the museum has 25 of his pieces), Picasso and Braque, to the vibrant new generation of Danish installation artists. There is a children's section on the ground floor of the new wing, with plenty of hands-on action on offer. The museum also has a notable café/restaurant. See also p82.

>COPENHAGEN DIARY

Copenhagen keeps things fairly low key as far as festivals and celebrations go. Aside from the justly famous Copenhagen Jazz Festival and the extravagance of Christmas, the city resists much public hullabaloo. Nevertheless, visitors can still enjoy a packed calendar of events to suit all tastes. The best sources for up-to-date info on events are www.aok.dk and www.visitcopenhagen.com. Once in Copenhagen, seek the free listings paper *Copenhagen This Week* (actually a monthly), the Danish-language *Citadel* and the English-language *Copenhagen Post*.

In November, the old central square of Kongens Nytorv transforms into a giant skating rink

JANUARY & FEBRUARY

New Year

On the last day of the year many Copenhageners let rip with extravagant, hour-long fireworks displays. These tend to be private events with precious few safety concerns, although there are also some public displays. Thousands congregate in front of the town hall on Rådhuspladsen for the big moment.

Winter Jazz Festival

www.vinterjazz.dk

From the end of January to early February those suffering from jazz withdrawal after the midyear jazz festival can get their fix from this smaller-scale festival held at various venues through the city.

MARCH

Natfilm Festival

www.natfilm.dk

This atmospheric 'night film' festival is held throughout the city's cinemas during the second half of March. This is Denmark's largest film festival, showcasing over 160 new movies from around the world.

Bakken

www.bakken.dk

Denmark's oldest fun park opens on the last weekend in March in the forested deer park of Dyrehaven (p69).

A roar of approval for the fun rides at Bakken

Royal guards march to Amalienborg Slot on Dronning Margrethe II's Birthday

APRIL

Dronning Margrethe II's Birthday

On April 16th, the much-loved Danish queen (p52) greets the crowds from the balcony of Amalienborg Slot at noon as soldiers in full ceremonial dress salute her. Thousands flock to pay their respects and even the city buses fly flags in celebration.

Tivoli

www.tivoli.dk

The historic city-centre amusement park (p92) reopens in mid-April for its summer season with a new programme of events and concerts, usually including several major international names. The first day is usually packed but the season lasts until the end of the third week in September.

MAY

Labour Day

Workers of the world unite in Fælledparken for union-led picnics, boozing, song and dance. It is not officially a national holiday but is pretty much treated like one!

Ølfestival

www.haandbryg.dk

Specialist beer and microbrewing are booming in Denmark right now. This is the country's largest beer festival, drawing crowds of over 10,000 thirsty attendees.

COPENHAGEN DIARY

Brazilian-style shebang with floats, musicians and costumed dancers.

Samba rhythms at the Copenhagen Carnival

JUNE

Skt Hans Aften (St Hans Evening)
The Danes let rip on the longest night of the year with bonfires in parks, gardens and, most popular of all, on the beaches. They burn an effigy of a witch on the pyre (she is said to fly off to the Hartz mountains in Germany), sing songs and get merry.

Roskilde Festival
www.roskilde-festival.dk
Scandinavia's largest music festival takes place in fields just outside the town of Roskilde, around half an hour by train from Copenhagen. Roskilde draws major international acts and crowds of over 80,000 music lovers from around the world. See also p20.

Copenhagen Marathon
www.sparta.dk
Scandinavia's largest marathon is on a Sunday in mid-May and draws around 5000 participants and tens of thousands of spectators.

Copenhagen Carnival
www.karneval.dk
Held over three days at Whitsun (50 days after Easter) this is the Danes' take on a

Copenhagen Distortion
www.cphdistortion.dk
A five-day celebration of the city's nightlife, held in early June, with the emphasis on clubs and DJ bars.

Danish Derby
www.galopsport.dk
Denmark's most important horse race is held in late June at the Klampenborg racecourse to the north of the city.

JULY

Copenhagen Jazz Festival

www.jazzfestival.dk

Copenhagen's single largest event, and the largest jazz festival in northern Europe, is held over 10 days in early July. The festival celebrates jazz in all its forms, featuring world-class singers and musicians. This carnival of street performances really brings the city to life; see also p157.

AUGUST

Kulturhavn (Culture Harbour)

www.kulturhavn.dk

This unique event, held during the first week of August, focuses on the harbour and waterways of Copenhagen with a wide programme of cultural events, sports and parades, centred on the recently redeveloped 'beach' at Islands Brygge (p48). Most events are free.

Index

www.indexawards.dk

As befitting one of the great design capitals of the world, Copenhagen now has its own annual design event, Index, centred on a 100-entry strong annual design award and held from mid-August to late-September. Entrants are usually exhibited in pavilions in the city's main squares.

Jazz on the water at the Copenhagen Jazz Festival

Glitter, glamour and good times at the Copenhagen Pride parade

Copenhagen Cooking

www.copenhagencooking.dk

Scandinavia's largest food festival focuses on the gourmet end of the food spectrum and is held in venues and restaurants throughout the city – though centred on Øksnehallen – from the end of August to early September.

Copenhagen Pride

www.copenhagenpride.dk

This popular gay and lesbian parade transforms the city centre throughout the day and well into the small hours, with much dancing, flirting and camping. Lots of fun.

SEPTEMBER

Golden Days Festival

www.goldendays.dk

This cultural-historic festival takes place every two years (the next are in 2008 and 2010) for three weeks from early September and involves many museums and venues in the city. The theme is different each time – the 2006 festival focused on King Christian IV and the Renaissance.

Buster

www.buster.dk

This thriving children's film festival runs for one week in mid-September and features offerings from around the world, plus workshops where children can make their own films.

Art Copenhagen

www.artcph.com

This major art fair showcases the work of over 450 Nordic artists and attracts over 10,000 visitors.

Copenhagen Blues Festival

www.copenhagenbluesfestival.dk

This international event is held over a week in late September at various venues in the city.

Copenhagen Film Festival

www.copenhagenfilmfestival.dk

Featuring 100% European films (dominated by Danish entries), this relatively new festival held over 10 days in late September shows 145 films, often with director/actor Q&As.

OCTOBER

Kulturnatten (Culture Night)

www.kulturnatten.dk

Usually held on the second Friday in October, this wonderful, atmospheric event sees the city's museums, theatres, galleries, libraries and even Rosenborg Slot throw open their doors through the night, with a wide range of special events. Public transport is free this night.

NOVEMBER

CPH:Dox

www.cphdox.dk

This acclaimed international documentary film festival, now in its fifth year and the largest of its kind in Scandinavia, screens films in several cinemas throughout the city from early to mid-November.

Soaking up the atmosphere of Kulturnatten at Thorvaldsens Museum (p103)

The warm glow of Christmas in Rådhuspladsen

DECEMBER

Great Christmas Parade

Copenhagen kicks off one of its favourite
times of the year with a parade that
works its way through the city centre on the
last Saturday in November. Father Christmas
and his *nisser* (elves) enter the city
amid much ballyhoo, ending up in
Rådhuspladsen for the lighting of the
giant tree.

Tivoli

www.tivoli.dk

Tivoli reopens from mid-November to 23
December for Christmas with a large market
and buckets of schmaltz. Attractions include

special Christmas tableaux, costumed
staff and theatre shows. Fewer rides are
operational but the mulled wine and
æbleskiver (small doughnuts) ought to be
ample compensation. See p92.

Christmas

Copenhageners really go to town at this
time of year. The shopping streets and
shop fronts are extravagantly decorated,
Christmas markets pop up around town and
there are church concerts galore. The entire
frontage of the Hotel d'Angleterre (p59) is
transformed with a spectacular Christmas
scene that changes every year. Danes
celebrate Christmas at home on the evening
of the 24th with a traditional dinner and
dancing round the tree.

Dronning Luises Bridge, Nørrebro

ITINERARIES

ONE DAY

Start at Statens Museum for Kunst (p82), then wander through the serene gardens of Kongens Have (p81) and past Rosenborg Slot (p82) to Kongens Nytorv (p51). Cross the square to Nyhavn for a late-morning beer (p62) then explore the small, boutiquey streets of Store Strandstræde and Lille Strandstræde behind (p55). After lunch at Ida Davidsen (p59) head back to Kongens Nytorv and then down Strøget (p104), perhaps stopping to browse in the interior design temple, Illums Bolighus (p117). End up at Rådhuspladsen (p88), where it's a short walk to Tivoli (p92). Finish the day with a hearty dinner at The Paul (p95).

TWO DAYS

Begin at the Ny Carlsberg Glyptotek (p90) before heading across the road to the Dansk Design Center (p90). On nearby Strædet you will find a marvellous array of smaller, independent antique, fashion and homeware stores (p112). Stop for lunch at Zirup (p126). At Amagertorv, turn right across to Slotsholmen, dominated by Christiansborg Slot (p100), but also home to the Thorvaldsens Museum (p103) and Det Kongelige Bibliotek (p101). Cross the harbour to Christianshavn (p40) and wander beside the canals here. See if you can pick up a ticket for a performance at the Opera House (p49), or spend the evening at Noma restaurant (p47).

THREE DAYS

Explore Istedgade (p131) before heading back to Halmtorvet, with its alfresco cafés and restaurants for lunch. Across from here is the exhibition space Øksnehallen (p131), or you could relax with one of the many beauty or health treatments at DGI-Byen (p136) just around the corner. Take the S-train from Central Station to Nørreport (p78). Head north and you can explore trendy Nansensgade or head on across the city lakes to Nørrebro (p64) and the shops on Ravnsborggade and Elmegade (p67). Party the night away at Gerfärlich (p75) and then Rust (p77) or, from Sundays to Tuesdays, enjoy a quieter dinner at one of the cafés or restaurants nearby (see p70).

Top left Detail of Frederik VII statue and the spire of Børsen (p100) **Top right** Thorvaldsens Museum (p103), Slotsholmen **Bottom** Shopping for the latest fashions at Strøget (p112)

ITINERARIES

Getting to know Copenhagen via the canals of Nyhavn

SUNNY DAY
Start with a swim at the harbour pool at Islands Brygge Havnebadet
(p48). Wander the canals of Christianshavn and Christiania (p42), aiming
for lunch at Restaurant Kanalen (p48). Take the Harbour Bus (p173) from
Knippelsbro to Nyhavn (p50) and walk from there to the Little Mermaid
(p54), followed by a tour around the ramparts of Kastellet (p53). From
here you can walk virtually across the top of the city centre using only its
parks – Østre Anlæg connects to Botanisk Have, from where it is a short
hop to Ørsteds Parken (p80). End the day with alfresco sushi at Sticks 'n'
Sushi (p84) on nearby Nansensgade.

RAINY DAY
Slotsholmen has Christiansborg Slot (p100), Thorvaldsens Museum
(p103), Tøjhusmuseet (p103), Teatermuseet (p103), Kongelige Stalde
(p101) and Kongelige Bibliotek (p101), all close together (although you

FORWARD PLANNING

In keeping with its generally relaxed, informal vibe, a trip to Copenhagen doesn't require much planning but a little organisation can still help. Buy tickets for the Opera House (p49) and Royal Theatre (p62) well in advance, for instance, and check out www.aok.dk (Alt om København, 'All About Copenhagen') and www.visitcopenhagen.com for news of other upcoming entertainment and events, and for tickets contact www.billetnet.dk or www.billetlugen.dk. If Mette Martinussen's private dinner party restaurant, 1.th (p57) takes your fancy you will need to book three weeks in advance; the same goes for many of the city's Michelin-starred restaurants, as well as some of the better-value, fixed-menu places like Les Trois Cochons (p133) or Famo (p132). A week before, visit www.ctw.dk (Copenhagen This Week) and www.aok.dk. You can subscribe to the aok.dk newsletter – it's in Danish but you should be able to get the gist. If you'd like to take a walking tour, book at least a week ahead; the same goes for Dine With the Danes (p134). A day before you go, buy and print a ticket for Tivoli at www.tivoli.dk to avoid sometimes lengthy queues.

hould note that they are not all open on the same days). You can have unch in the café at the Bibliotek, or at the more expensive Søren K resaurant (p103) looking out at the harbour. From here it's umbrellas ahoy or a quick dash to Nationalmuseet (p90) and, afterwards, a cosy coffee r something stronger in front of the open fire at Petit Delicé (p123). In he evening, the Vega complex (p136) has all your nightlife needs under ne roof.

COPENHAGEN ON THE CHEAP

Vednesday is the best day to do things on the cheap. Start at Statens Museum (p82). Pop round the corner to Den Hirschsprungske Samling free on Wednesdays; p80), and then across Kongens Have to the Davids amling (always free; p80). Pick up a city bike (p171) and cycle to Chrisiania (p42) for a curry lunch at Morgenstedet (p47). Every Wednesday students from the Danish Music Conservatorium stage free classical conerts (see www.onsdagskoncerter.dk – in Danish only, but easy to follow), t various venues around the city. Alternatively, every Friday, included in he admission, is a live music performance at Tivoli (p92), often by a maor international act. For dinner try Lê Lê Nhà Háng (p133) in Vesterbro.

Bars and restaurants alongside the canals of Nyhavn (p50)

NEIGHBOURHOODS

The great joy of a visit to Copenhagen is that most of the major sights and shops are all within easy reach of each other.

The city's pavements are broad, the cycle paths are religiously respected and it is as flat as a billiard table. Given a relaxed programme and a stout pair of shoes you can easily take in all of the city on foot or by bike over three or four days. Alternatively, you can let the excellent bus, harbour bus and metro systems whisk you about the place, and cram even more in.

Copenhagen began on the island of Slotsholmen 1000 years ago and this remains the political heart of Denmark. But today the city centre has expanded to include Rådhuspladsen and Tivoli, where you also find the main concentration of hotels; the pedestrian shopping area, Strøget, and its fascinating side streets; and the royal area north of Nyhavn, stretching to the Little Mermaid, and including the current royal residence, Amalienborg Slot. Look at a map of the city and, broadly, you can see that its heart is contained within the borders formed by HC Andersens Blvd to the west of the city centre, the city lakes to the north, and the harbour, which curves from the east round to the south. Most of the conventional sights – museums, monuments, major shops, sights and restaurants – remain within these areas.

But, of course, museums and posh shops are only part of what Copenhagen has to offer. Beyond the historic centre lie exciting, vital areas that are well worth visiting: the canal quarter, Christianshavn, to the east of the harbour; vibrant Vesterbro and romantic Frederiksberg to the west; the area north of Nørreport Station with its mix of interesting shops, nightlife and sights; and beyond that, to the northwest and northeast, the buzzing nightlife and hip shopping area, Nørrebro, and the embassy quarter, Østerbro.

ØRESUND

1 km
0.5 miles

NØRREBRO
& ØSTERBRO
(p65)

NØRREPORT
TO ØSTERPORT
(p79)

NYHAVN TO
KASTELLET
(p51)

STRØGET
& AROUND
(pp106-7)

VESTERBRO &
FREDERIKSBERG
(p129)

SLOTSHOLMEN
(p99)

RÅDHUSPLADSEN
& TIVOLI
(p89)

CHRISTIANSHAVN
AND ISLANDS
BRYGGE
(p41)

Yderhavnen

Inderhavnen

Sydhavnen

Peblinge Sø

Sortedams Sø

>CHRISTIANSHAVN & ISLANDS BRYGGE

Historic canals, quirky churches, 18th-century town houses, and leafy city ramparts combine to make Christianshavn one of Copenhagen's prettiest quarters. This is mostly a residential area, home to not-really-struggling artists, yuppies doing their best to look relaxed and bohemian, and a large Greenlandic community. Slap-bang in the middle of it all, like some quarrelsome, elderly relative who everyone tries to ignore, is Christiania (p42), the 'alternative community' founded in an army barracks in 1971. Further northeast of here is Holmen, formerly a naval base and industrial area, now home to the Danish Film and Architecture schools, costly waterside apartments and the magnificent new Opera House (p49).

On the other side of Amager Boulevard from Christianshavn, to the south, is one of Copenhagen's upcoming areas, Islands Brygge, which has a striking harbour swimming pool (p48). Islands Brygge really comes alive during the summer when it serves as a kind of inner-city beach, albeit one without sand. Come here in the winter, however, and you might wander what all the fuss is about…

CHRISTIANSHAVN & ISLANDS BRYGGE

SEE

CHRISTIANIA

☎ 32 95 65 07; www.christiania.org; Prinsessegade; Ⓜ Christianshavn ☐ 66
The dream of a self-sufficient, utopian society rooted in the free love and chemical indulgence of the late 1960s may have turned sour in recent years. The police have clamped down on the open sale of soft drugs but drug-related violence has actually increased since, and there appears to be quite an alcohol problem here. But the sheer 'otherness' of the Christiania lifestyle guarantees an eye-opening experience for visitors, nonetheless. The main entrance is located on Prinsessegade, 200m northeast of its intersection with Bådmandsstræde. There is a small market selling the usual Camden Town tat on the right, as well as a couple of café-restaurants and genuine craftsmen elsewhere on the site. You can take a guided tour of Christiania with a local resident. Tours meet just inside the main entrance at 3pm on weekends, during the warmer months. See also p13.

CHRISTIANS KIRKE

☎ 32 54 15 76; Strandgade 1, admission free; ⏰ 8am-6pm Sun-Thu, 8am-5pm Fri & Sat; Ⓜ Christianshavn ☐ 350S, 2A, 66, 19, 47, Harbour bus Knippelsbro
Nicolai Eigtved's theatre-like church was completed in 1759.

WORTH THE TRIP

Amager Strandpark (Ⓜ Lergravsparken, then ☐ 12) is a sandy-sational manmade lagoon, 10 minutes from Christianshavn on the coast road to the airport. The beach has room for hundreds of sun-worshippers and bathers and is a popular water-sports destination. There are cafés and bars here in the summer, with wonderful views of the Øresund Bridge. A new metro station is due to open here, close to the northern end of the beach, in 2008.

Meanwhile, the small but pristine **Bellevue beach** (S-train Klampenborg) at the heart of the 'Danish Riviera', 20 minutes to the north of the city, throngs with body-beautifuls in the summer. There is an excellent Franco-Danish gourmet restaurant, **Den Gule Cottage** (€€€€; ☎ 39 64 06 91; www.dengulecottage.dk; Strandvejen 506, Klampenborg; ⏰ noon-4pm, 6pm-midnight Mon-Sat; S-train Klampenborg), located in a twee, half-timbered cottage on the grassy hill overlooking the beach.

Looking further afield, virtually the entire northern coast of Zealand is made up of time-warp fishing harbours and glorious sandy beaches, two of the best being at **Gilleleje** and **Hornbæk** (both reachable with an hour-and-a-half by train from Helsingør).

Christianshavn's art is not just restricted to its galleries

This is a frequent venue for classical music recitals (leaflets at the entrance to the church provide details).

☒ GAMMEL DOK
☎ 32 57 19 30; www.dac.dk; Strandgade 27B; exhibition adult/concession/child 40/25kr/free; ⏰ 10am-5pm; Ⓜ Christianshavn ☒ 350S, 2A, 66, 19, 47; ♿

Home to the Dansk Arkitektur Center, this converted 19th-century warehouse offers changing exhibitions on Danish and international architecture, as well as an excellent bookshop.

☒ OVERGADEN
☎ 32 57 72 73; www.overgaden.org; Overgaden Neden Vandet 17; 1-5pm Tue-Sun; Ⓜ Christianshavn ☒ 350S, 2A, 66, 19, 47

Rarely visited by tourists, this tucked-away gallery mounts challenging exhibitions of contemporary installation art and photography, usually by younger artists.

COPENHAGEN FOR FREE

Copenhagen has a reputation for being a costly city, but many of its top sights are free for at least one day of the week. The following items are free all week unless a particular day is specified.

> Assistens Kirkegård (p66)
> Christiania (p42)
> Churches, including Marmorkirken (p54) and Vor Frelsers Kirke (below)
> Davids Samling (p80)
> Den Hirschsprungske Samling (free on Wednesday only; p80)
> Folketinget (p102)
> Frihedsmuseet (p53)
> Kastellet (p53)
> Københavns Bymuseet (free on Friday only; p130).
> Nationalmuseet (p90)
> Ny Carlsberg Glyptotek (free on Sunday only; p90)
> Opera House lobby (p49)
> Statens Museum for Kunst (p82)
> The Little Mermaid (p54)
> Thorvaldsens Museum (free on Wednesday only; p103)
> Tøjhusmuseet (free on Wednesday only; p103)

⊙ VOR FRELSERS KIRKE (CHURCH OF OUR SAVIOUR)

☎ 32 57 27 98; Sankt Annæ Gade 29; admission free, tower adult/child 20/10kr; ☽ 11am-4.30pm Mon-Sat, noon-4pm Sun; Ⓜ Christianshavn ☐ 350S, 2A, 66, 19, 47

The extraordinary spire is the main draw at this 17th-century church close to Christiania (p42). It takes a strong resolve to climb all the way to the top, 400 steps and 95m up, as the last 150 steps run around the *outside* of the tower, narrowing to the point where they literally disappear. The tower was added to the church in 1752 by Lauritz de Thurah, who took his inspiration from Boromini's tower of St Ivo in Rome.

🛍 SHOP

🛍 ANDERSEN S COMPANY GALLERY *Art*

☎ 46 97 84 37; www.andersen-s.dk; Islands Brygge 43; ☽ noon-5pm Tue-Fri, 11am-3pm Sat; ☐ 34

Located in the heart of arty Islands Brygge, this gallery represents some of the biggest names in Danish art, including Olafur Eliasson.

Camilla Berner
Artist

Best place for a social drink Our local café, Café Wilder (p46). **Where to spot up-and-coming Danish artists** The degree show at the Kunstforeningen (p108) is good, as are the exhibitions at Charlottenborg (p52), or you could visit some of the new galleries in Islands Brygge (opposite). **Top art spaces** Louisiana (p66) is always worth a look. More centrally and perhaps less mainstream, Overgaden (p43) is my favourite. **Venue for a birthday treat** Noma (p47). **Copenhagen's hidden secret** If you go to Christiania, keep walking away from the main areas, down to and along the water and you'll find some quite fantastic architecture. **If you're here short-term, make sure you go to** Christianshavn. **Favourite shop** Stilleben (p120), a tiny shop in Læderstræde with ceramics and glass by Danish and international craftspeople.

🏛 GALLERI NICOLAI WALLNER GALLERY *Art*
☎ 32 57 09 70; www.nicolaiwallner
.com; Njalsgade 21, Building 15, Islands
Brygge; noon-5pm Tue-Fri, noon-3pm Sat;
Ⓜ Islands Brygge 🚌 12, 33, 34
This unprepossessing gallery
houses some top-notch Scandinavian and international artists.
A genuine Islands Brygge pioneer.

🍴 EAT

🍴 ARISTO
Mediterranean €€
☎ 32 95 83 30; www.cafearisto.dk;
Islands Brygge 4; 🕙 11am-midnight
Mon-Thu, 11-2am Fri, 10-2am Sat,
10am-11pm Sun; 🚌 5A, 12, 33, 40,
250S, 34; ♿
At the heart of pulsating Islands
Brygge is this airy, contemporary
café-restaurant serving pretty,
modern Danish and Italian cuisine
such as *quail pot au feu* (gently
simmered quail), or *pork tenderloin saltimbocca* (filled pork rolls).

🍴 BASTIONEN OG LØVEN
Danish €€
☎ 32 95 09 40; www.bastionen-loven.
dk; Christianshavns Voldgade 50; 10am-
midnight; 🚌 350S, 2A, 66, 19, 47
This charming café-restaurant is
housed beside a historic windmill
on the city ramparts just south of
Christiania. Its front garden is the
perfect place to enjoy a classic
Copenhagen brunch – cheese,
smoked salmon, omelette, pan-
cakes, fresh fruit, yoghurt, bacon,
coffee, juice etc – on a sunny
Sunday morning.

🍴 CAFÉ WILDER *Café*
€
☎ 32 54 71 83; www.cafewilder.dk;
Wildersgade 56; 🕙 9am-midnight Mon,
9am-1am Tue & Wed, 9am-2am Thu &
Fri, 9.30-2am Sat, 9.30am-midnight Sun;
Ⓜ Christianshavn 🚌 350S, 2A, 66, 19,
47; ♿
This friendly, laid-back corner café
in the heart of Christianshavn
serves pasta salads and sandwiches by day and more substantial

WHEN IS A DANISH NOT A DANISH
Wherever you go in Denmark the bakeries tend to stock the same range of syrupy, buttery,
nut-sprinkled pastries with perhaps a dab of jam or custard in the middle. To the rest of the
world they are known as 'Danish pastries' but ask for 'a Danish' in a *bageri* in Copenhagen
and the baker will probably give you a funny look and perhaps direct you to the brothels
of Istedgade. The Danes call them *wienerbrød* (literally 'Vienna bread') and, true to their
collective sweet tooth, they eat them for breakfast. A quick look in the history books tells
us that *wienerbrød* is the more appropriate name as this style of cake originated in Austria
in the 18th century.

Franco-Danish food by night. It is one of the most popular cafés in the area, especially with the well-chilled arty community.

🍴 LAGKAGEHUSET *Bakery* €

☎ 32 57 36 07; www.lagkagehuset.dk; Torvegade 45; 6am-7pm; Ⓜ Christianshavn 🚌 350S, 2A, 66, 19, 47; ♿

This much-loved bakery – recently voted the best in the city – sells excellent sandwiches as well as the usual sticky, sweet pastries and heavyweight rye bread.

🍴 MORGENSTEDET *Vegetarian* €

Langgade, Christiania; 🕙 noon-9pm Tue-Sun; Ⓜ Christianshavn 🚌 66

A homely-hippy little place in the heart of the alternative commune of Christiania, Morgenstedet offers but one dish of the day, always vegetarian, always organic, usually a curry and always at a bargain price.

🍴 NOMA *Modern Nordic* €€€€

☎ 32 96 32 97; www.noma.dk; Strandgade 93; 🕙 noon-2.30pm, 6pm-midnight Mon-Fri, 6pm-midnight Sat; 🚌 350S, 2A, 66, 19, 47; ♿

This renowned, Michelin-starred Modern Nordic restaurant is run by chef Rene Redzepi (formerly of Le Bulli and The French Laundry), who uses only Scandinavian-sourced produce like musk ox, smoked eel

Docked for a dinner at Noma

and locally caught lobster and oysters, with a classically-orientated, European-centric wine list. Not the most exciting ambience perhaps, but it could well be the most exciting food in Denmark.

🍴 SPISELOPPEN *Global* €€

Langgade, Christiania; ☎ 32 57 95 58; dinner Tue-Sun; Ⓜ Christianshavn 🚌 66

Christiania's evening offering is this ambitious dinner restaurant situated in the Loppen building. Spiseloppen serves up a global menu – the cuisine depends on the nationality of the kitchen's chef on the night!

RESTAURANT KANALEN
Franco-Danish €€-€€€

☎ 32 95 13 30; www.restaurant-kanalen .dk; Wilders Plads 2; ⏱ 11.30am-3pm, 6pm-midnight Mon-Sat; 🚌 350S, 2A, 66, 19, 47; ♿

You can eat in this lovely, unpretentious gourmet restaurant beside the canal watching the yacht masts ticking like metronomes, and pretend you are in St Tropez…kind of. Well, at least you can enjoy great Danish staples like smørrebrød (p17) for lunch and more classically French inspired dishes, such as Danish lamb with *Pommes Anna* (a butter-rich potato gratin), for dinner.

VIVA *Global* €€

☎ 27 25 05 05; www.restaurant-viva.dk; Langebrogade Kajplads 570; ⏱ 11.30am-3pm & 5.30pm-midnight Mon-Thu, 11.30am-3pm & 5.30pm-1am Fri & Sat, 5.30-9pm Sun; 🚌 5A, 12, 33, 40, 250S

A kind of floating version of Aura (p121), this unique restaurant, on board a ship moored beside Langebro, has the same team behind it and a similarly inventive menu of tapas-sized, modern European dishes.

🍸 DRINK
🍸 SOFIE KÆLDEREN
DJ/Jazz Bar

☎ 32 57 77 01; www.sofiekaelderen .dk; Over Gaden Oven Vandet 32; noon-midnight Tue & Wed, noon-3am Thu-Sat, 10am-10pm Sun; Ⓜ Christianshavn, 🚌 350S, 2A, 66, 19, 47

This former old-school jazz bar in a cellar beside the canal is now a cool live-music venue and lounge, serving globally-influenced food for lunch and dinner.

⭐ PLAY
❏ ISLANDS BRYGGE HAVNEBADET *Swimming*

☎ 23 71 31 89; Islands Brygge, beside Langebro; admission free; 7am-7pm 1 Jun-31 Aug; 🚌 5A, 12, 33, 40, 250S, 34

This has to be the funkiest public swimming pool (designed by trendy architects Plot) you'll ever see. It takes some courage to plunge into the waters of Copenhagen harbour, though they do at least test it regularly for cleanliness. If you don't fancy a swim, there are lawns, skateboarding parks, basketball courts, restaurants and cafés where you can chill out on a sunny day. It has a real carnival atmosphere during the summer holidays.

Opera lovers flock to the Copenhagen Opera House

LOPPEN *Live Music*

☎ 32 57 84 22; www.loppen.dk; Christiania; ⏰ 9pm-2/3am; admission varies
free-140kr; Ⓜ Christianshavn 🚌 66
This historic, timbered warehouse
in Christiania doesn't draw quite so
many major international acts as it
used to but is still one of the best
live-music venues in the city –
everything from punk to reggae,
funk and world music can be heard
here, usually followed by a boisterous disco into the early hours.

COPENHAGEN OPERA
HOUSE *Live Music*

☎ 33 69 69 69; www.operaen.dk;
Ekvipagemestervej 10; box office ☎ 33
69 69 69; ⏰ noon-6pm Mon-Sat; tickets
0-690kr, 50% discount under 25s and over
65s; 🚌 66 & Harbour bus Operaen; ♿

This state-of-the-art opera
house features two stages, the
Main Stage and a smaller venue,
Takkeløftet. The repertoire runs
the gamut from classic to contemporary opera, as well as the odd
curve ball like a performance by
Elvis Costello or something from
the Jazz Festival (p157). Productions usually sell out way in advance but 25 tickets are available
each day at the box office. To get
valid discounts, you need to book
more than a week in advance.
Alternatively, many come just to
look around the building or eat in
the panoramic Franco-Danish restaurant or ground-floor café. There
are guided tours on Saturday and
Sunday at 9.30am and 4.30pm
(100kr).

>NYHAVN TO KASTELLET

The colourful Dutch-style town houses that line the historic Nyhavn canal are one of the city's most photographed sights. Built in the 17th century to link the harbour to the city centre, today the canal is lined with popular, rather touristy bars and restaurants. On warmer, rain-free days, the cobbles are crowded with people downing a beer or two.

North of Nyhavn is Copenhagen's royal quarter, Frederiksstaden, where you will find the four palaces that make up Amalienborg Slot (p52) – the Danish royal family's main residence – as well as Marmorkirken (p54). Frederiksstaden stretches to Churchill Park, home to the Frihedsmuseet (p53) and the ancient city fortress, Kastellet (p53). Beside Kastellet, overlooking the harbour, is one of the city's most anticlimactic sights, the Little Mermaid (p54).

NYHAVN TO KASTELLET

👁 SEE

🔵 AMALIENBORG SLOT

☎ 33 12 21 86; www.rosenborg-slot.dk;
Amalienborg Plads; adult/child 45/10kr;
🕙 10am-4pm 1 May-31 Oct, 11am-4pm
Tue-Sun 2 Jan-30 Apr & 1 Nov-30 Dec;
🚌 1A, 15, 19; ♿

Amalienborg is made up of four rather staid 18th-century palaces ranged around a large cobbled square. It has been home to the Danish royal family since 1794. If you enter the square from the harbour to the east, the palace on your left is the home of the current queen, Margrethe II. Copenhagen's one great photo opportunity, the changing of the guard, takes place here every day at noon after the new guard has paraded through the city centre from its barracks beside Rosenborg Slot (p82). Across the square in another palace is the Amalienborg Museum, which recreates various royal rooms from the 19th century to WWII. The Danes are fervent royalists and love this kind of stuff, but this is perhaps not going to be of great interest to overseas visitors.

🔵 CHARLOTTENBORG

☎ 33 13 40 22; www.charlottenborg
-art.dk; Nyhavn 2; 🕙 10am-5pm Mon &
Tue, Thu-Sun, to 7pm Wed; adult/conces-
sion 30/15kr; Ⓜ Kongens Nytorv, 🚌 15,
19, 26, 1A; ♿

This large, red-brick building is the historic home of the Kongelige

MARGRETHE THE MARVELLOUS

One of the great paradoxes of this most democratic of societies is that its people are so unquestioningly devoted to their monarch. But Dronning Margrethe II is no ordinary monarch. She became queen – in the wake of a national referendum permitting women to succeed the throne – upon the death of her father in 1972 and was the first female Danish monarch since the 14th century. She is an undeniably excellent ambassador for the country, remains regal (unlike, say, the cycling Dutch royal family) and is a talented artist. Margrethe has illustrated a number of books, designed sets for the Royal Theatre and translated Simone de Beauvoir texts into Danish. She also chain-smokes, which is guaranteed to endear her to her countrymen. Her consort is the French-born Henrik, a mildly comic figure in Danish society. Together they have two children, the widely adored Crown Prince Frederik, who married a Tasmanian, Mary Donaldson, in 2004, and the slightly less-loved Joachim (who divorced his Hong Kong-born wife, Alexandra, in the same year). Frederik and Mary remain the fairytale couple – dashing, beautiful and jetsetting – with many glamorous celebrity friends and an enviable life composed of foreign jaunts and sporting pleasures (both are keen sailors and horsey-types). They have one son, Christian, and one daughter, affectionately named *'lille pige'* (little girl) until her christening in July 2007. Europe's oldest monarchy looks to be in safe hands.

Kunstakademi (The Royal Academy of Fine Arts). It is one of the best venues to see contemporary Danish and international art, with changing exhibitions through the year.

FRIHEDSMUSEET
☎ 33 13 77 14; www.natmus.dk; Churchillparken; admission free; 10am-3pm Tue-Sun Oct-Apr, to 5pm Tue-Sun May-Sep; 🚌 1A, 15, 19, Harbour bus Nordre Toldbod; ♿

This small museum charts the exploits of the Danish resistance during the occupation by the Germans in 1940, to liberation by the British in 1945. Exhibits include moving letters written by resistance fighters awaiting execution, uniforms and sabotage equipment.

KASTELLET
🚌 1A, 15, 19; ♿

The star-shaped fortress of Kastellet was originally commmissioned by Frederik III in 1662. Today it is one of the most historically evocative sites in the city. Its grassy ramparts and moat surround some beautiful 18th-century barracks, a chapel (sometimes used for concerts) and a tiny lifeguards museum (by the southern gate). On the ramparts is a historic windmill and some excellent views to the Little Mermaid, the harbour and, in the other direction, Marmorkirken.

Vibrant textiles at Kunstindustrimuseet

KUNSTINDUSTRIMUSEET
☎ 33 18 56 56; www.kunstindustri museet.dk; Bredgade 68; adult/child 50kr/free; 11am-5pm Tue-Sun; 🚌 1A, 15, 19; ♿

One of Copenhagen's loveliest museums boasts an impressive collection of decorative arts, including extensive displays of European and oriental furniture, silverware and porcelain, with an emphasis on 20th-century Danish design. It's housed in a former hospital built around a courtyard in 1752. It's a wonderful spot to spend a rainy afternoon and there is an inviting café. Check out the Drud & Køppe gallery (p56), whose entrance is in the front courtyard.

THE LITTLE MERMAID

Love it or loathe it, when the world thinks of Copenhagen the statue of the Little Mermaid is the one of the first things that springs to mind. Unfortunately, many do seem to loathe this tiny statue of one of Hans Christian Andersen's most famous characters, which was created by sculptor Edvard Eriksen in 1913 and paid for by the Carlsberg Brewery. She has been vandalised repeatedly, losing her head and her arms on a couple of occasions. In 2006 Danish artist Bjørn Nørgaard was commissioned by Carlsberg (among others) to create a new Little Mermaid. He came up with a 'genetically altered' mermaid that sits not far from the original beside the harbour and is, in fact, probably truer in spirit to the rather bleak, twisted Andersen fairy tale. Unlike the Disney version, of course, Andersen's mermaid suffers all manner of physical and emotional torments, and definitely doesn't get her man.

MARMORKIRKEN

☎ 33 15 01 44; www.marmorkirken
.dk; Frederiksgade 4; admission free,
dome adult/child 20/10kr; ⏱ 10am-5pm
Mon-Thu, noon-5pm Fri-Sun, dome 1pm
& 3pm Sat & Sun Sep-mid Jun, 1-3pm
mid-Jun-Aug; 🚌 1A, 15, 19

The Marble Church, or to give it its correct name, Frederikskirken, is one of the most imposing pieces of architecture in the city and, we might add, a perhaps more fitting symbol for the Danish capital than the winsome Little Mermaid. Its dome was inspired by St Peter's in Rome and measures more than 30m in diameter. The original plans for the church were ordered by Frederik V and drawn up by Nicolai Eigtved. Construction began in 1749 but, as costs spiralled and the Danish economy foundered, the project was mothballed. It wasn't until Denmark's wealthiest financier, CF Tietgen, agreed to finance the church in the latter part of the

19th century that construction began again. You can climb up to the dome at weekends; the views to Sweden are stunning. Do note that the church closes for weddings and funerals.

Head for the imposing dome of Marmorkirken

The Little Mermaid, with emphasis on the 'little'

SHOP

The main areas of interest for shoppers here are stately Bredgade, which is home to the auction houses and high-end antique and art dealers; Store Kongensgade, which runs parallel to Bredgade to the north and has a broader range of independent high-street shops and restaurants; and Store Strandstræde and Lille Strandstræde, which lie behind Nyhavn to the north and have several chic boutiques.

MEDICINSK-HISTORISK MUSEUM

☎ 35 32 38 00; www.mhm.ku.dk; Bredgade 62; adult/concession 30/20kr; ⏱ guided tours 11am & 1pm Wed-Fri, 1pm Sun Sep-Jun, 1pm Sun Jul-Aug; 🚌 1A, 15, 19

This fascinating, if occasionally gruesome, museum housed in a former teaching hospital covers the history of medicine, pharmacy and dentistry. It's all rather chilling, with plenty of pickled body parts and grisly diagrams. The original teaching theatre, where hundreds of cadavers have been dissected over the years, has an especially ghoulish atmosphere. Guided tours are conducted in English.

BANG & OLUFSEN
Electronics

☎ 33 11 14 15; www.bang-olufsen.com; Kongens Nytorv 26; ⏱ 10am-6pm Mon-Thu, to 7pm Fri, to 4pm Sat; Ⓜ Kongens Nytorv 🚌 15, 19, 26, 1A; ♿

The flagship store for the world-famous Danish audio-visual brand sells its distinctive, sleek, exquisitely designed TVs, stereos and other electrical equipment.

BITTE KAI RAND
Fashion

☎ 33 11 99 30; www.bittekairand.dk; Lille Strandstræde 22; ⏱ 10am-5.30pm Mon-Thu, to 5pm Fri, to 4pm Sat; 🚌 15, 19, 26, 1A

Ask many Copenhagen women over 30 for one of their favourite addreses and the name of this veteran of the Danish fashion scene will invariably crop up. Rand presents six collections a year of sophisticated, chic and very, very beautiful clothing.

DRUD & KØPPE *Art*
☎ 33 33 00 87; www.drud-koppe.com; Bredgade 66; 🕐 11am-5.30pm Tue-Fri, to 3pm Sat; 🚌 1A, 15, 19

A remarkable gallery of amusing, intriguing, frustrating and eye-opening contemporary art awaits behind the unassuming door to this new gallery, just off the courtyard entrance to Kunstindustrimuseet. Curators Birgitte Drud and Bettina Køppe assemble regularly changing collections of one-off or limited edition contemporary pieces by leading local artists as well as international guest artists. Tends towards more playful, commercial pieces.

GALERIE ASBÆK *Art*
☎ 33 15 40 04; www.asbaek.dk; Bredgade 20; 11am-6pm Mon-Fri, to 4pm Sat; Ⓜ Kongens Nytorv 🚌 1A, 15, 19

Martin Asbæk has been at the centre of Copenhagen's contemporary art establishment for over 30 years and represents top local artists as well as some major names from overseas. He also sells slightly more affordable books and posters.

KLASSIK MODERNE MØBELKUNST *Furniture*
☎ 33 33 90 60; www.klassik.dk; Bredgade 3; 🕐 11am-6pm Mon-Fri, 10am-3pm Sat; 🚌 1A, 15, 19

This showroom, close to Kongens Nytorv, is the largest on Bredgade and features a trove of Danish design classics from the likes of Poul Henningsen, Hans J Wegner, Arne Jacobsen, Finn Juhl and Nanna Ditzel – in other words, a veritable museum of Scandinavian furniture from the mid-20th century.

SANDWICH *Fashion*
☎ 33 11 34 20; www.veldhoven group.com; Store Strandstræde 19; 🕐 10.30am-6pm Mon-Thu, to 7pm Fri, to 4pm Sat; 🚌 15, 19, 26, 1A

This inviting store is one of severa women's clothes and jewellery

BEST DESIGN STORES

> Designer Zoo (p131) – studio and showroom for local young designers
> Illums Bolighus (p117) – design superstore
> Casa Shop (p115) – major international furniture design and the hottest interior styles
> Dansk Design Center shop (p90) – excellent for design gifts
> Klassik (above) – Bredgade's one-stop shop for classic Danish design from the 20th century

Some of the finest contemporary Danish design can be found at Illums Bolighus (p117)

stores on this charming side street off Nyhavn. It sells casual and dressy women's clothes from this popular Dutch design group.

🎩 SUSANNE JUUL *Hats*

☎ 33 32 25 22; www.susannejuul .dk; Store Kongensgade 14; 🕐 11am-5.30pm Tue-Thu, to 6pm Fri, to 2pm Sat; Ⓜ Kongens Nytorv 🚌 15, 19, 1A

If you are looking for a hat that makes a statement, or something more discreet, this is the place to come. Perhaps the best milliners in the city, with prices ranging from 500kr to 5000kr.

🍴 EAT

🍴 1.TH

Modern European/Danish €€€€

☎ 33 93 57 70; www.1th.dk; Herluf Trolles Gade 9; 🕐 invitation only, evenings Wed-Sat; Ⓜ Kongens Nytorv, 🚌 15, 19, 26, 1A

This unique, private dining 'restaurant' is housed in a classic Copenhagen apartment. 1.th translates as 'first floor, to the right' – the location of this sumptuously decorated living and dining room, open to guests of chef Mette Martinussen. You reserve and pay the 1100kr bill (which includes wine) well in advance, then receive an invitation to a convivial, soirée-style evening with a multicourse dinner as the main attraction. Highly recommended, and the contemporary Danish-European food lives up to the high concept.

🍴 CAP HORN
Danish €€-€€€

☎ 33 12 85 04; www.caphorn.dk; Nyhavn 21; 🕑 9am-1am (kitchen closes at 11pm); Ⓜ Kongens Nytorv 🚌 15, 19, 26, 1A

Few places really stand out on Nyhavn but this is a perennial favourite. Cap Horn is more refined than some of the other places here

and serves accomplished Franco-Danish food with a good range of smørrebrød at lunch. There's an open fire in winter that turns the *hygge* (p154) meter up to '11'.

🍴 EMMERYS *Bakery* €

☎ 33 13 01 33; www.emmerys.dk; Store Strandstræde 21; 🕑 7.30am-6.30pm Mon-Thu, 7.30am-6.30pm Fri, 8am-5pm Sat & Sun; 🚌 15, 19, 1A; ♿

This sophisticated, trendy bakery, coffee shop and delicatessen chain has branches throughout Copenhagen (in Nørrebro, Vesterbro and Østerbro) selling its own brand of coffee, as well as

Stop for a beer and smørrebrød at the refined Cap Horn

cakes, muffins, bread, wine and chocolate. Irresistible and high up on the list of locals' favourites for a weekend treat.

🍴 ENSEMBLE
Modern Danish   €€€€

☎ 33 11 33 52; www.restaurant ensemble.dk; Tordenskjoldsgade 11; ⏰ dinner Tue-Sat; Ⓜ Kongens Nytorv 🚌 15, 19, 26, 1A

Chefs Morten Schou and Nikolaj Egebøl-Jeppesen had a tough act to follow when they took over what was a successful Michelin-starred restaurant a couple of years ago, but their artful and inventive Modern Danish cooking has succeeded in maintaining the reputation of this intimate restaurant's reputation (and its star). Located in a quiet residential street behind the Kongelige Teater (p62), Ensemble's menu blends local ingredients – root vegetables, wild game, shellfish – with French haute cuisine staples like foie gras and truffles. Typical dishes include eel with apple, quails eggs, brioche and chervil, or coquelet with foie gras, salsify and salad.

🍴 IDA DAVIDSEN *Danish*   €

☎ 33 91 36 55; www.idadavidsen.dk; Store Kongensgade 70; ⏰ 10am-4pm Mon-Fri; 🚌 15, 19, 1A

The queen of smørrebrød (see also p17).

🍴 PRÉMISSE
Modern Danish/French   €€€€

☎ 33 11 11 45; www.premisse.dk; Dronningens Tværgade 2; ⏰ noon-2pm & 6pm-midnight Mon-Fri, dinner only Sat; Ⓜ Kongens Nytorv 🚌 15, 19, 1A

A sublime culinary experience is guaranteed in this vaulted cellar restaurant in a historic mansion. Chef Rasmus Grønbech takes the sourcing of the finest Danish ingredients for his restaurant very seriously, applying classic French techniques, learned during stints at Michelin restaurants, with dedication and wit. Meanwhile, sommelier Christian Aarø Mortensen is a champion wine steward with an exceptional list (it's particularly strong on Spanish wines).

🍴 RESTAURANT D'ANGLETERRE
French   €€€-€€€€

☎ 33 37 06 45; www.remmen.dk; Hotel d'Angleterre, Kongens Nytorv 34; 7am-10pm Mon-Thu & Sun, to 11pm Fri & Sat; Ⓜ Kongens Nytorv 🚌 15, 19, 26, 1A D

Copenhagen's hotel restaurants are not usually terribly appealing, but the five-star Hotel d'Angleterre's is a cut above, serving alluring classic French cuisine built upon a solid foundation of the best Danish raw ingredients, and served in a glamorous, glistering dining room overlooking Copenhagen's grandest square.

Lissen Marschall
Singer

Best place to hear live jazz Vega (p136) is really special, but don't forget Tivoli (p92) has some great concerts. **Top tip for someone new to Copenhagen** Walk everywhere – it is the only way to see the city. **Where do you go to buy clothes** Elmegade (p67) has loads of really great clothing stores, small, independent designers for quite reasonable prices. **Other favourite shopping places** I can spend days in the antique shops on Ravnsborggade (p67) and Bredgade (p55). **Favourite restaurant** If it's a money-no-object night out, then Prémisse (p59), if I'm in a glamorous mood, Umami (opposite), or if I just want something quick and cheap, Lê Lê (p133) on Vesterbrogade does really great Vietnamese food.

🍽 SALT
Modern Danish/French   €€-€€€

☎ 33 74 14 48; www.saltrestaurant.
dk; Toldbodgade 24-28; 🕒 noon-4pm &
5pm-midnight; 🚌 29; 🚹

A converted 18th-century corn
warehouse is the beautiful venue
for this Terence Conran–designed
(yes, him again) Modern Danish/
French hotel restaurant close to the
site of the new theatre. Seafood,
local organic meats and game are
regulars on an ambitious menu
that might include confit of monk-
fish, crisp fried crab with pome-
granate or roast rack of rabbit.

🍽 TASTE *French Café*   €

☎ 33 93 77 97; www.cascabel.dk; Store
Kongensgade 80-82; 🕒 9.30-5pm Mon-
Thu, 9.30-6pm Fri, 11am-4pm Sat; 🚌 15,
19, 1A; 🚹

Just around the corner from
Marmorkirken is this delectable
French-owned deli-takeaway-café
serving mostly organic, homemade cakes, bread, salads, choco-
lates and salad along with the best
muffins in Copenhagen.

🍽 THE CUSTOM HOUSE
Global   €€-€€€

☎ 33 31 01 30; www.customhouse.dk;
Havnegade 44; 🕒 11.30am-midnight
Mon-Wed & Sun, to 1am Thu, to 2am Fri &
Sat; 🚌 29, Harbour bus Nyhavn; 🚹

Sir Terence Conran's recently
opened gourmet complex is

housed in the old ferry terminal,
where boats used to embark for
Sweden. As well as a small deli,
there are three appealing upscale
(or should that be 'Yuppiescale'?)
restaurants here. At Bacino
the menu is contemporary but
authentic Italian, with dishes including *langoustine* (shrimp) with
pumpkin risotto or fillet of halibut
with basil, courgette and almond
cream. Ebisu serves what is for
Copenhagen an unusually wide
range of Japanese dishes, while
the Grill Bar apes a more casual,
upmarket New York steak joint.
The food and service varies from
excellent to so-so but, as you'd
expect, the décor is smooth and
sophisticated, with lots of dark
stained wood and slate.

🍽 UMAMI
Japanese-French   €€-€€€

☎ 33 38 75 00; www.restaurantumami
.dk; Store Kongensgade 59; 🕒 noon-
3pm, 6-11pm Mon-Sat; 🚌 15, 19, 1A; 🚹

This glamorous restaurant, over-
seen by chef Francis Cardenau and
designed by Orbit of London like
some kind of *Wallpaper* fantasy,
sees classic French cuisine flirt
heavily with modern Japanese
cooking (saddle of rabbit served
with wasabi and soy, for example)
to usually sensational effect. It is
at its best in the evenings and at
weekends when the DJ does his
thing.

NEIGHBOURHOODS

NYHAVN TO KASTELLET

🍴 WOKSHOP CANTINA
Asian   €

☎ 33 91 61 21; www.wokshop.dk; Ny Adelgade 6; 🕑 noon-2pm, 5.30pm-midnight Mon-Fri, noon-2pm, 6pm-10pm Sat. Ⓜ Kongens Nytorv 🚌 15, 19, 26, 1A
This great-value, Wagamama-style modern Thai place is close to Kongens Nytorv and to the rear of Hotel d'Angleterre.

🍴 ZELESTE *Global*   €€

☎ 33 16 06 06; www.zeleste.dk; Store Strandstræde 6; 🕑 11am-midnight; 🚌 15, 19, 26, 1A
If the restaurants on nearby Nyhavn don't appeal, this excellent, globally influenced restaurant featuring exotic ingredients like *pata negra* ham and Argentinian beef on its menu (they like to describe themselves as 'con-fusion cooking' is a good alternative. In summer be sure to request a table outside in the pretty courtyard to the rear.

🍸 DRINK

🍸 FISKEN *Pub*

☎ 33 11 99 06; Nyhavn 27; 🕑 11.30am-11pm; Ⓜ Kongens Nytorv 🚌 15, 19, 26, 1A
This open-all-hours cellar pub beneath the atmospheric Skipper Kroen restaurant distils the essence of everything great about Nyhavn's salty sea-dog atmosphere, with nightly live folk music

🍸 PALÆ BAR *Pub*

☎ 33 12 54 71; Ny Adelgade 5; 🕑 10-1am Mon-Wed, 10-2am Thu-Sat, 4pm-1am Sun; Ⓜ Kongens Nytorv 🚌 15, 19, 26, 1A
This cosy, old-school drinking den is popular with an older crowd of journalists, writers and politicians.

⭐ PLAY

🎭 DET KONGELIGE TEATER (THE ROYAL THEATRE) *Theatre*

☎ 33 69 69 69; www.kglteater.dk; Kongens Nytorv; Ⓜ Kongens Nytorv 🚌 15, 19, 26, 1A ♿
Opera and theatre productions are still performed at the beautifu

---

THE HOMES OF HANS CHRISTIAN ANDERSEN

Despite earning great wealth in later life, Hans Christian Andersen never owned his own home but instead rented apartments at three addresses on Nyhavn during his life – first at No 20, where he began writing the stories that would make him world famous, then for 17 years at No 67 and finally at No 18. This restless traveller, who journeyed as far as Istanbul and North Africa and who many believe was homosexual, loved to watch the life of the canal and feel as if he were in touch with the world across the sea. Although, the sailors down below might also have been part of the appeal... (see also p93).

Statue of a poet outside Det Kongelige Teater

world-class productions from the Royal Danish Ballet. The current building, the fourth theatre to occupy the site, was completed in 1872 and was designed by Vilhelm Dahlerup and Ove Petersen. The statues by the steps are of Ludvig Holberg, the 18th-century playwright, and Adam Oehlenschläger, the national poet. Tickets for productions here usually sell out well in advance but 25 tickets are sold at a discount of 50% each day from the **box office** (☎ 33 69 69 69; ⊙ noon-6pm Mon-Sat).

⭐ SKUESPILLER HUSET
Theatre

Kvæsthusgade; 🚌 **29** ♿

At the time of writing Denmark's impressive new theatre, designed by Boje Lundegaard and Lene Tranberg, was due for completion on reclaimed land on the harbour front at Kvæsthusbroen by the end of 2007. When finished it will have two stages – a 750-seater and a 250-seater – and will be clad in copper and crowned by a set tower. It ought to look rather stunning. At that point theatre productions will move here from the Kongelige Teater (opposite).

historic 'old stage' here on Kongens Nytorv, but with the arrival of the new Opera House on Holmen (p49) and the imminent new Playhouse Theatre (Skuespiller Huset) on the harbour front, the mainstay here will eventually be

>NØRREBRO & ØSTERBRO

Nørrebro and Østerbro are chalk-and-cheese neighbours: one cool, lively, ethnically diverse and edgy, the other sedate, family-orientated and a little smug. Nørrebro started off as a working-class neighbourhood and now has a large immigrant community. As well as hosting the occasional riot (the most recent example being the violent and prolonged demonstration against the closing of a well-established squat, Ungdomshuset, in March 2007), Nørrebro is one of the most delectable nightlife destinations in the city and it is also a cutting-edge fashion centre.

Østerbro, or the 'embassy quarter', has some good midrange shopping, restaurants and the city's largest park, Fælledparken (p67), home to the national stadium, Parken (p77).

Nørrebro and Østerbro lie to the northwest and northeast of the city centre respectively, stretching from the eastern Vesterbro/Frederiksberg border to Nordhavn, the northern harbour.

NØRREBRO & ØSTERBRO

SEE

ASSISTENS KIRKEGÅRD

☎ 35 37 19 17; Kapelvej 4, Nørrebro; admission free; ⏲ 8am-5pm 1 Jan-28 Feb, to 6pm 1 Mar-30 Apr & 1 Sep-31 Oct, to 8pm 1 May-31 Aug, 8am-4pm 1 Nov-31 Dec; 🚌 5A, 350S; ♿

This leafy cemetery in the heart of Nørrebro is the burial place of some of Denmark's most celebrated citizens including Hans Christian Andersen, his old foe Søren Kierkegaard and physicist Niels Bohr. The main entrance is on Kapelvej. You should be able to pick up a map at the office here.

EXPERIMENTARIUM

☎ 39 27 33 33; www.experiment arium.dk; Tuborg Havnevej 7, Hellerup; ⏲ 9.30am-5pm Mon & Wed-Fri, to 9pm Tue, 11am-5pm Sat & Sun; 12 yrs & over 125kr, child 3-11 80kr, child 0-2 free; 🚌 14 from Rådhuspladsen to the neares stop, Tuborg Blvd; ♿

This frenetic, dizzying museum is dedicated to inspiring children's interest in nature, technology, the environment and health. This is a genuinely exciting, hands-on experience and kids adore it. As wel as all the permanent experiments there is a changing programme o temporary themed exhibitions – previous ones have included dinosaurs, robots and Sports & Spinach. This 4100 sq m museum opened in 1991 and is located a little north of the city centre, alon the coast, in the old brewery harbour beside the poshest suburb i the city. There is a café and shop on site.

WORTH THE TRIP

Louisiana Museum for Modern Art (☎ 49 19 07 19; www.louisiana.dk; Gammel Strand-vej 13, Humlebæk; adult/child 80kr/free; ⏲ 10am-5pm Thu-Tue, to 10pm Wed; 🚌 Humlebæk) is one of the finest modern art museums in Scandinavia. As well as world-class art from the constructivist, pop art, nouveau realist and other movements, the museum also has an elegant concert hall with regular Friday classical concerts, a café with outdoor seating alongside lawns that stretch down to the sea and a vibrant children's section. Along with the permanent collection, the museum also offers six to eight temporary exhibitions each year – check the website for details. These temporary exhibitions draw huge crowds, particularly at weekends. The original manor house, dating from 1855, has been extended over the years and is situated on the outskirts of the affluent coastal town of Humlebæk, 35km north of Copenhagen. It is 36 minutes by train from the Central Station and another 10 minutes on foot to the museum (there are signposts – you turn left once you reach the main road in front of Humlebæk station). See also p14.

All hands on hard hats at the Experimentarium

SHOP

The main shopping streets in Nørrebro are Nørrebrogade itself, a busy, local shopping street; Blågårdsgade, just off it to the west, which has a couple of nice cafés and fashion stores; and Elmegade, the trendy heart of the area – indeed of the city – where some of the hippest clothing stores rub shoulders with sushi and bagel places. Nearby Ravnsborggade is the best place in the city for vintage jewellery, kitschy furniture and antiques – although the bric-a-brac and antique shops are increasingly being pushed out by new men's and women's fashion stores these days.

Østerbrogade is Østerbro's main shopping street, with Nødre Frihavnsgade another good bet. Apart perhaps from Normann (p70) there aren't really any shops that make a visit to Østerbro worthwhile in themselves, but there is a good mix of midrange shops here if you feel like a change from Strøget and its environs.

☐ ANTIKHALLEN *Antiques*

☎ 35 35 04 20; Sortedams Dossering 7C, Nørrebro; ☽ 3-6pm Mon-Fri, 11am-3pm Sat; ☒ 5A, 350S

One of the best antique furniture and bric-a-brac shops in this excellent antique area, with a wide range of styles and periods.

◉ FÆLLEDPARKEN

🚌 42, 43, 150S, 15, 1A; ♿

Copenhagen's largest park is a functional, if not especially attractive, open space popular with amateur footballers. It is dominated by the giant concrete monolith of Parken (p77), the national stadium.

◉ ZOOLOGISK MUSEUM

☎ 35 32 10 01; www.zoologiskmuseum .dk; Universitetsparken 15, Østerbro; adult/child 60/25kr; ☽ 10am-5pm Tue-Sun; 🚌 42, 43, 150S, 184, 185, 18; ♿

Copenhagen's zoological museum is popular with kids, with its interesting display of stuffed animals, sealife and birds.

🖼 FAJANCERIET *Ceramics*

☎ 35 35 26 50; www.fajanceriet
.dk; Birkegade 1, Nørrebro; ⏱ noon-
5pm Tue-Thu, to 3pm Fri & Sat; 🚌 5A,
350S, 3A

This adorable contemporary
ceramic shop stocks the
highly collectible work of local
designers and is located just off
Elmegade.

🖼 FREDERIKSEN *Fashion*

☎ 35 35 05 66; Ravnsborggade 15, Nørrebro; ⏱ 11am-6pm Tue-Fri, 11am-3pm
Sat; 🚌 5A, 350S, 3A

Lise Frederiksen's super-feminine
clothing boutique is just one of
several new fashion shops on
what used to be thought of as the
city's top antiques street. She is
joined by Dico, Stig P, Riktigt and
the groovy gift shop Kiertner (all
located on Ravnsborggade) in the
ongoing trendification of this area

🖼 FROGEYE *Footwear*

☎ 35 37 01 39; Blågårdsgade 2a, Nørrebro; ⏱ 10am-6pm Mon-Thu, to 7pm
Fri, to 4pm Sat; 🚌 5A, 350S, 3A

This is one of the grooviest shoe
shops in the city, with a wide

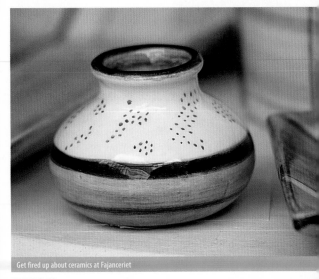

Get fired up about ceramics at Fajanceriet

WORTH THE TRIP

Dyrehaven (Klampenborg; S-train Klampenborg; &) is a 1000-hectare former royal hunting ground (think Richmond Park, without the traffic) much loved by joggers, cyclists, rollerbladers and picnickers (it is also the best place to bring a toboggan when there's snow). You can drive – though there is not much parking – via the coast road to Klampenborg. The turning for the park entrance is on the left (if you are coming from the city) just after Bellevue Beach (on your right) and Arne Jacobsen's celebrated Bellevue theatre and apartment complex (on your left). But it is quicker by train – just 22 minutes from the Central Station. Klampenborg Station is right beside the main gate to the park.

Dyrehaven is also home to the 1538-founded **Bakken** (☎ 39 63 35 44; www.bakken .dk; Dyrehavevej 62, Klampenborg; admission free, rides individually priced; ☺ 2-10pm Mon-Wed, to midnight Thu & Fri, 1pm-midnight Sat, noon-10pm Sun end Mar-last week May, 2pm-midnight Mon-Fri, 1pm-midnight Sat, noon-midnight Sun end May-last week Jun, noon-midnight end Jun-1 Aug, 2pm-midnight Mon-Fri, 1pm-midnight Sat, noon-midnight Sun 2 Aug-20 Aug; S-train Klampenborg, then 800m walk), which is said to be the world's oldest amusement park. The cynical might say it looks it, but if you approach it in the right frame of mind (admittedly, a couple of beers and some candy floss helps), Bakken can be a lot of fun. This is very much an old-school funfair experience, with creaking 1970s rides, tame rollercoasters, appalling fast food and cheesy cabarets. There are about 100 rides in all, as well as 35 cafés and restaurants.

ange of Camper footwear always n stock.

FÜNF *Fashion*
☎ 33 37 13 80; www.funf.dk; Elmegade 2, Nørrebro; ☺ 11am-6pm Mon-Fri, to 8pm Sat; 🚌 5A, 350S, 3A
This gorgeous women's clothing store on trendy Elmegade stocks up-to-the-second ranges from several local designers. There are several of these kind of slightly edgy fashion boutiques nearby, including Goggle, Resteröds, Bark, Cappalis and, just around the corner on Guldbergsgade, Weiz.

KLÆDEBO *Fashion*
☎ 35 36 05 27; Blågårdsgade 3, Nørrebro; ☺ noon-6pm Mon-Fri, 10.30am-2pm Sat; 🚌 5A, 350S, 3A
The best fashion shop on this interesting pedestrian street just off Nørrebrogade sells stylish, modern and trendy women's and children's clothes.

MAYOL *Gifts/Homeware*
☎ 35 36 01 39; www.mayol.dk; Blågårdsgade 5, Nørrebro; ☺ noon-6pm Mon-Thu, noon-7pm Fri, 10am-4pm Sat; 🚌 5A, 350S, 3A
This is the kind of small, independent shop that Copenhagen does

really well. It stocks irresistible gifts and knick-knacks for the home, kitchen, office and bathroom.

🏠 NORMANN
Homeware/Furniture/Fashion

☎ 35 55 44 59; www.normann
-copenhagen.com; Østerbrogade 70,
Østerbro; 🕙 10am-6pm Mon-Fri, to 3pm
Sat; 🚌 1A, 14, 15; 🚻

This recently opened, 1700-sq-metre clothing and interior design store is housed in a vast, whitewashed room – formerly a cinema – on Østerbro's main shopping street. As well as stocking its own award-winning brand of homewares (including the famous rubber washing-up bowls, collapsible 'Funnel' strainer, stemless cognac glasses and outlandish cardboard lampshades), Normann also stocks vintage-style sportswear, furniture and Alessi homewares, and clothing byJoseph and Resteröds. Think of

it as a more cutting-edge Illums Bolighus (p117).

🍴 EAT

🍽 ATAME *Spanish*   €

☎ 35 35 12 30; www.atame.dk;
Blågårdsgade 3, Nørrebro; 🕙 11am-
10pm Mon-Sat, noon-10pm Sun; 🚌 5A,
350S, 3A

This is an excellent-value Spanish tapas bar and takeaway based in a small cellar, and is enduringly popular with the locals.

🍽 AUBERGE
Franco-Danish   €€–€€€

☎ 35 35 39 00; www.cofoco.dk;
Østerbrogade 64; 🕙 5.30pm-midnight;
🚌 1A, 14, 15

This sexy basement restaurant, with its trendy raw brick/glass-walled décor is run by the Cofoco group (p132). The food is slightly more refined Franco-Danish, multicourse dishes in which the

---

WORTH THE TRIP

Architect Zaha Hadid's sexy, slinky glass and stone extension put **Ordrupgaard** (☎ 39 64 11 83; www.ordrupgaard.dk; Vilvordevej 110, Charlottenlund; adult/child 70/55kr; Tue & Thu-Fri 1-5pm, 10am-6pm Wed, 11am-5pm Sat & Sun; S-train to Klampenborg, then 🚌 388; 🚻) on the international map when it opened in 2005. However, this charming art museum, housed in a pretty, early-20th-century manor house to the north of Copenhagen, has always had an enviable collection of 19th- and 20th-century art. Works include paintings by Gauguin (who lived in Copenhagen for many years), Renoir and Matisse, as well as notable Danish artists of that period such as JT Lundbye and Vilhelm Hammershøj. There is a nice café here, too, with outdoor seating in summer.

A stunning fusion of food styles is served at Bodega

two-course starter and three-course 'main course' are each variations on one ingredient (raw and grilled scallops for the starter, for instance, and duck confit, pan-fried and breaded, for the main).

BODEGA Global   €-€€

☎ 35 39 07 07; www.bodega.dk; Kapelvej 1, Nørrebro; 🕙 10am-midnight Tue, to 2am Wed & Thu, to 4am Fri & Sat, to 11pm Sun; 🚊 5A, 350S

This recently renamed and re-invigorated DJ bar-café-restaurant beside the walls of Assistens Kirkegård (p66) is one

of the hotspots in this hottest of neighbourhoods. The fresh-thinking fusion kitchen is accomplished and soul, funk and R&B grooves are spun from Thursday to Saturday nights.

DAG H Franco-Danish   €€

☎ 35 27 63 00; www.dagh.dk; Dag Hammarskjölds Allé 36-40; 🕙 8am-11pm Mon-Thu, to midnight Fri, 10am-midnight Sat, to 10pm Sun; 🚊 1A, 14, 15; ♿

Formerly the coffee temple Amokka, Dag H now takes the name of the street on which it stands and remains the prime weekend brunch destination (when it is best to book in advance) for the locally resident young professionals with kids in tow. One of the city's larger cafés, it boasts a beautiful, contemporary interior and plenty of outdoor seating in summer with a short but predictable menu of French brasserie classics, burgers, fancy sandwiches and salads (their three-course evening menu for 250kr is a good deal). Kontra Coffee next door is the city's best coffee-making equipment store.

FRU HEIBERG
Franco-Danish €€

☎ 35 38 91 00; Rosenvængets Allé 3, Østerbro; 🕒 5-11pm Tue & Wed, 10-2am Thu-Sat, to 11pm Sun; 🚌 1A, 14, 15
What used to be an old-fashioned Greek restaurant is now one of the most popular restaurants in Østerbro, serving contemporary Franco-Danish food and run by the people behind Gefärlich (p75). It is a lovely, cosy place invariably packed to the rafters with young diners and drinkers at the weekends, when booking is advised.

KAFFESALONEN
Franco-Danish €€

☎ 35 35 12 19; Pebling Dossering 6, Nørrebro; 🕒 8am-midnight Mon-Fri, 10am-midnight Sat & Sun; 🚌 5A, 350S

This lovely café-restaurant is right beside the city lakes – actually, make that on the city lakes as, during the summer, it moves out to a floating deck. Perfect for a sundowner.

PUSSY GALORE'S FLYING CIRCUS *Global* €-€€

☎ 35 24 53 00; www.pussy-galore.dk; Sankt Hans Torv 30, Nørrebro; 🕒 8am-2am Mon-Fri, 9am-2am Sat & Sun; 🚌 5A, 350S, 3A; ♿
This Sankt Hans Torv pioneer remains popular, thanks to a great location on the quarter's most buzzing square, with plenty of outdoor tables and a clever, good value fusion menu.

🍸 DRINK

If you are looking for bars and clubs catering to a relaxed, predominantly 20s and early-30s crowd, make a beeline for Nørrebro.

CAFÉ BOPA *DJ Bar*

☎ 35 43 05 66; www.bopa.dk; Løgstørgade 8, Østerbro; 🕒 10am-midnight Mon-Wed & Sun, to 2am Thu, to 5am Fri & Sat; S-train Nordhavn Station; 🚌 1A, 14
This quiet square in the heart of a residential part of the city throbs to DJ-spun beats at the weekend as Bopa pumps up the volume and turns into one of the city's best flirty venues.

There's always something brewing at Nørrebro Bryghus

☎ NØRREBRO BRYGHUS
Brewery

☎ 35 30 05 30; www.noerrebrobryghus
.dk; Ryesgade 3, Nørrebro; ⏰ 11am-
midnight Mon-Wed & Sun, to 2am
Thu-Sat; 🚌 3A, 5A, 350S

This two-storey brewery with a
lounge bar and good, midrange
restaurant kickstarted the microbrewing craze in Denmark a few
years back (master brewer Anders
Kissmeyer looks after the beer
side of things) and the concept
remains as fresh and alluring as
ever.

☎ OAK ROOM *Bar*

☎ 38 60 38 60; Birkegade 10, Nørrebro;
⏰ 7pm-midnight Tue, to 2am Wed &
Thu, 5pm-2am Fri, 7pm-2am Sat; 🚌 3A,
5A, 350S

If we had to nominate one place
to go for a memorable, flirty,
drunken Copenhagen evening
right now, it would have to be the
Oak Room. This sweaty, minimalist, invariably packed two-room
cocktail bar is close to trendy
Elmegade and just around the
corner from Rust (p77).

TEA TIME Tearoom

☎ 35 35 50 58; www.tea-time.dk; Birkegade 3, Nørrebro; ☽ noon-8pm Mon, 9am-8pm Tue-Fri, 10am-5pm Sat & Sun; ▣ 3A, 5A, 350S

An improbable but welcome addition to Nørrebro's edgy, underground scene is this quaint English tearoom. Expect homemade cupcakes, pink lemonade, fine teas and finger sandwiches, all served with just a hint of postmodern irony. This is the kind of place that just makes your day better. They also have a branch just off Istedgade.

THE LAUNDROMAT CAFÉ Café

☎ 35 35 26 72; Elmegade 15, Nørrebro; ☽ 8am-midnight Mon-Thu, to 2am Fri, 10-2am Sat, to noon Sun; ▣ 5A, 350S, 3A

This playful corner café was the brainchild of Icelander Fridrik Weisshappel who decided to turn the old Morgans juice bar into a

Do your washing, read a book or just catch up with friends at The Laundromat Café

WORTH THE TRIP

Said to be one of the finest Renaissance palaces in Northern Europe, **Frederiksborg Slot** (☎ 48 26 04 39; www.frederiksborgslot.dk; Hillerød; ⏰ 11am-3pm Nov-Mar, 10am-5pm Apr-Oct; adult/concession/child 60/50/15kr; S-train Hillerød, 40 min north of Copenhagen, then 10-min walk through town centre; ♿) was bought by Frederik II in 1560 from a local nobleman. By rights, 'Christiansborg' Slot would be a better name, as Christian IV was both born here in 1577 and built the castle that stands today in its red-brick and sandstone splendour in the Dutch Renaissance style. Following a devastating fire in 1859, the castle was rebuilt using funds from the Carlsberg Foundation and opened as the Museum of National History in 1877, filled with a priceless collection of furniture and art.

café-laundrette, with washing machines just round the corner from the bar (wonder where he got that idea from?). Throw in 4000 secondhand books (all available to purchase) to decorate the bar and you have one of Copenhagen's most distinctive and enjoyable venues.

⭐ PLAY

🔲 DANSESCENEN *Dance*
☎ 35 43 83 00, box office 35 43 20 25; www.dansescenen.dk; Øster Fælled Torv 34, Østerbro; performance times vary, see website for details; 🚌 1A, 14, 15
This is Copenhagen's leading modern dance venue with 20 to 30 new, international-standard productions each year.

🔲 GEFÄRLICH *Club*
☎ 35 24 13 24; Fælledvej 7, Nørrebro; ⏰ 11am-midnight Tue, 11-2am Wed,

11-3am Thu, 11-3.30am Fri, 10-3.30am Sat, 10-1am Sun; 🚌 1A, 14
This deeply groovy bar/club/restaurant/lounge/café/hairdresser/clothing store/art space (really) has made a major splash on the Nørrebro nightlife scene. It gets packed at weekends, with the incriminating evidence usually posted on its My Space page by midweek.

🔲 PARK CAFÉ *Club*
☎ 35 42 62 48; www.parkcafe.dk; Østerbrogade 79, Østerbro; admission varies; ⏰ 11am-midnight Mon & Sun, to 2am Tue & Wed, to 5am Thu-Sat; 🚌 1A, 14
It may not be cutting edge in terms of the music policy and clientele's dress sense (miaow!), but this large, dressy bar/nightclub is always popular and has a couple of dancefloors – one of which often plays host to live music.

⭐ **Stephan Sander**
Web Designer

Favourite place to meet with friends for a drink Gefärlich (p75) on Fæll
vej is a nice place to sit outside with a drink on a summer's day, listening
classic jazz. Either there or The Laundromat Café (p74) on Elmegade – a v
cosy, crowded and entertaining place. Very Nørrebro. **Favourite lunch sp**
The café at the top of the Post and Tele Museum (p123). The rooftop terra
is spectacular. **Venue for a birthday celebration** Famo (p132) on Saxoga
in Vesterbro. Excellent value for money and a relaxed, friendly atmospher
plus great food. **Copenhagen's 'secret treasure'** The heart of Nørrebro h
a lot to offer – everything from modern antiques to reasonably-priced me
and funky clothes. **If you're here for a short stop, make the effort to se**
The Harbour – it's what makes Copenhagen special.

Entertainment on a grand scale at Parken

⭐ PARKEN *Sports/Live Music*
Fælledparken, Østerbro; 🚌 1A, 14 D
Denmark's 22,000 seater (40,000 for concerts) national stadium hosts the city's top football team FCK, major sporting events and visiting rock and pop gods such as U2 and Robbie Williams.

⭐ RUST *Club*
☎ 35 24 52 00; www.rust.dk; Guld-bergsgade 8, Nørrebro; admission varies; 🕘 9pm-5am Wed-Sat; 🚌 3A, 5A, 350S; ♿
The edgiest of Copenhagen's major clubs, Rust has a reputation for spearheading new musical trends. There is a choice of spaces

here from nightclub to live-music hall and lounge, and an equally diverse musical policy. Over 21s only.

⭐ STENGADE 30 *Club*
☎ 35 36 09 38; www.stengade30.dk; Stengade 18, Nørrebro; 🕘 Tue-Sun times & admission vary; 🚌 3A, 5A, 350S
It may look a little rough and ready but this is one of the leading lights of the city's alternative scene. Stengade 30 showcases an eclectic mix of local DJs and musicians with everything from hip-hop and electronica to Berlin-style techno. Their Rub-a-Dub Sundays are legendary.

>NØRREPORT TO ØSTERPORT

Denmark is one of the few countries in the world where that hoary old travel-writing cliché 'land of contrasts' doesn't really apply. But this part of its capital, at least, has plenty of wildly different things to offer. On the one hand you have some of Copenhagen's flagship sights as well as the unexpected delights of the Hirschsprungske and Davids Samlingerne (collections). On the other hand, in the area centred on Nansensgade, you have a quietly hip quarter with intriguing boutiques, cool restaurants and laid-back bars.

The area is bordered to the north by the shallow city lakes, originally dug as a fire defence, and to the south by Voldgade, which becomes Øster Voldgade at the junction with Gothersgade. A small geographical liberty has been taken with a detour south (Nørreport really stops at Gothersgade, but it makes sense for the purposes of this guide) to take in Kongens Have and Rosenborg.

NØRREPORT TO ØSTERPORT

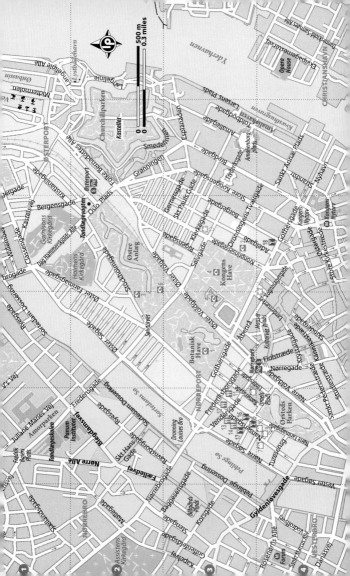

👁 SEE

📷 DAVIDS SAMLING

☎ 33 73 49 49; www.davidmus.dk; Kronprinsessegade 30; admission free; 🕐 1-4pm Tue & Thu-Sun, 10am-4pm Wed; 🚌 26, 350S

This jewel of a museum houses Scandinavia's largest collections of Islamic art (ironic, given the Mohammed cartoon furore of 2006; see p168), including jewellery, ceramics and silk, and exquisite works such as an Egyptian rock crystal jug from AD 1000 and a 500-year-old Indian dagger inlaid with rubies. That's all up on the 4th floor and worth a visit in itself but, on your way up, you can spend a fruitful couple of hours taking in the museum's fine Danish, English and French furniture and art from the 18th and 19th centuries. All of this was bequeathed to the museum by the barrister Christian Ludvig David, who died in 1960, and is maintained by his foundation. The museum is housed in his former home, a neoclassical mansion dating from 1806.

📷 DEN HIRSCHSPRUNGSKE SAMLING

☎ 35 42 03 36; www.hirschsprung.dk; Stockholmsgade 20; Thu-Tue adult/concession/child 50/40kr/free, Wed free; 🕐 11am-4pm Thu-Mon, to 9pm Wed; 🚌 14, 40, 6A, 42, 43; ♿

Giving Davids Samling a run for its money as the city's most underrated museum is tobacco magnate Heinrich Hirschsprung's collection of Danish art, most of it from the first half of the 19th century, and featuring some of the nation's most treasured paintings from its so-called 'Golden Age' (see p166). The museum displays moving and powerful works by the widely celebrated Funen and Skågen schools, famous for their haunting landscapes and depictions of 'ordinary' Danes and including

GARDEN STATE

This is not the most obviously picturesque place to wander – Nørre Voldgade and Øster Voldgade are big, wide, traffic-filled streets – but you can avoid them completely and walk almost the entire length of this part of the city through the beautifully landscaped gardens of Ørsteds Parken, Botanisk Have (Botanical Garden) and Østre Anlæg, the landscaped park behind Statens Museum for Kunst. In the summer months these parks throng with people enjoying picnics, reading in the sun or, in the case of Ørsteds Parken, a good number of gay men on the prowl. But the most popular of all is probably Kongens Have (Kings Park), to the south of Rosenborg, with its formal flower beds, children's puppet theatre and café.

Enjoying the Copenhagen summer in Kongens Have

artists such as Christen Købke, CW Eckersberg and PS Krøyer.

BOTANISK HAVE

☎ 35 32 22 40; www.botanic-garden.
ku.dk; Gothersgade 128; admission
free; ⏰ 8.30am-6pm May-Sep, to 4pm
Tue-Sun Oct-Apr; Ⓜ & S-train Nørreport,
🚌 6A, 184, 185, 150S, 173E

The beautiful Palmehus (Palm House) is the main attraction of this small but appealing botanic garden with 20,000 species of plants from around the world. A **Botanic Museum** (☎ 35 32 22 00; www .botaniskmuseum.dk; Gothersgade 130; admission free; ⏰ noon-4pm 19 Jun-31

Aug) features exhibits of plants from Denmark, Greenland and the rest of the world. There are two entrances to the garden: one at the intersection of Gothersgade and Øster Voldgade, and the other off Øster Farimagsgade.

KONGENS HAVE

Ⓜ & S-train Nørreport 🚌 350S, 6A, 184,
185; ♿

The oldest park in Copenhagen was laid out in the early 17th century by Christian IV, who used it as his vegetable patch. These days it has rather more to offer, including an excellent children's play area, beautiful flower beds and a marionette theatre with free performances during the summer holiday (2pm and 3pm, Tuesday to Sunday).

ROSENBORG SLOT

☎ 33 15 32 86; www.rosenborg-slot.dk; Øster Voldgade 4A; adult/child 50/40kr; ⏰ 11am-4pm Tue-Sun Jan-Apr, 10am-4pm May, 10am-5pm Jun-Aug, 10am-4pm Sep-Oct, 11am-4pm Nov–mid-Dec, closed mid-Dec–Christmas, 11am-4pm Dec 27-31; Ⓜ & S-train Nørreport, 🚌 350S, 6A, 184, 185, 150S

Copenhagen's stunning Renaissance Palace dates from the early 1600s. Its historic rooms, some of them decorative treasures in their own right, are full of artefacts and art from the royal collection. The crown jewels are in the basement while the carp that swim in the moat are said to have descended from Christian IV's pets/occasional dinner. See also p15.

STATENS MUSEUM FOR KUNST

☎ 33 74 84 84; www.smk.dk; Sølvgade 48; admission free; ⏰ 10am-5pm Tue & Thu-Sun, Wed to 8pm; Ⓜ & S-train Nørreport, 🚌 6A, 184, 185, 150S, 173E, 26; ♿

Denmark's impressive National Gallery (see p22).

A new Golden Age for the Copenhagen visual arts? Decide for yourself at the Statens Museum for Kunst

WHEN IN ROME

If you want to blend in with the locals, follow our essential 10-point plan:
> Smoke like a kipper
> Men – throw away your ties
> Women – throw away your bras
> Everyone – get on your bikes
> Throw away that extraneous top layer of bread, have smørrebrød for lunch (see p17)
> Wait for the green man before crossing
> Laugh at the Swedes
> Never serve salmon on brown bread
> Spend big on lampshades
> Don't queue for the bus – it's every man for himself!

SHOP

This is not a major shopping area but there are some cool designer boutiques on Nansensgade selling unique fashion clothing, accessories, retro homewares, gifts and 20th-century collectibles, and Frederiksborggade has a couple of outdoor pursuit stores (Spejder Sports at No 32; Fjeld & Fritid at No 28) catering to the climbing, walking and camping crowd.

CASIMOSE *Fashion*

☎ 33 13 61 63; www.casimose.dk; Nansensgade 35; ⏰ 10am-6pm Tue-Fri, to 3pm Sat; Ⓜ Nørreport 🚌 14, 40, 42, 43, 5A, 350S

Tina Casimose and Maiken Charlotte Bang offer one of the most consistent collections of womenswear on Nansensgade – the kind of clothing that is defining the Copenhagen look of today, with bold mix-and-match fabrics and patterns.

ISRAELS PLADS *Market*

⏰ early morning-5pm Mon-Fri, to 2pm Sat; 🚌 14, 42, 43, 184, 5A Ⓜ Nørreport

The Danish weather tends to deter outdoor produce markets, but the one on Israels Plads, close to Nørreport Station, has been going for decades. There is nothing special about the produce here – it sells mostly the same old Dutch peppers and industrial tomatoes you can get in the local supermarkets – but the prices are usually keener and there is nothing like buying your produce in the fresh air. The vendors might well disagree with us, however, as there are plans to turn it into a covered market by the end of 2007.

🖿 **MARIA & KENDT** *Fashion*
☎ 33 93 92 33; www.mariaandkendt.
dk; Nansensgade 42; ⏱ noon-6pm
Mon-Fri, 10am-2pm Sat; Ⓜ & S-train
Nørreport; 🚌 14, 40, 42, 43, 5A, 350S
This Swedish/Danish design duo
is making a name for itself in the
Danish fashion press for their light
(lots of chiffon and silk), girly, colourful partywear and more casual
clothing. Not cheap, but these are
limited runs.

🖿 **THE LAST BAG** *Bags*
☎ 46 92 73 90; www.thelastbag.dk;
Nansensgade 48; ⏱ 10am-4pm Tue-Fri,
11am-1pm Sat; 🚌 14, 40, 42, 43, 5A, 350S
This small shop has been selling the
same design of leather satchel – in
large and small and a variety of colours (red, black, white, light brown
and dark brown) – since 1954. If you
love timeless designs, this is one.

🍴 EAT
🍴 **CAFÉ KLIMT** *Global*   €-€€
☎ 33 11 76 70; www.cafeklimt.dk; Frederiksborggade 29; ⏱ 10am-midnight
Sun-Thu, to 3am Fri & Sat; Ⓜ Nørreport,
🚌 5A, 350S, 14, 40, 42, 43
This lively, one-room, candle-lit
'art café' has been popular for
several years now and is invariably
packed to the rafters with youngish locals delving into chef Bjørn
Vestergaard's (formerly of restaurant Hotel d'Angleterre) eclectic

MIND YOUR MANNERS
In Danish there is no direct equivalent
for the word 'please'. A polite request
is instead expressed by a tone of voice
and/or beginning a sentence with
phrases such as 'May I…' *(Må jeg…)*
or 'Could I…' *(Kunne jeg…)*.

global fusion menu of Cajun-Viet-
namese-Italian-wok food.

🍴 **KALASET** *Bar-Restaurant*   €
☎ 33 33 00 35; www.kalaset.dk; Vendersgade 16; ⏱ 11am-midnight Tue-Thu,
11-2am Fri, 10-2am Sat, 11am-11pm Sun;
🚌 5A, 350S, 14, 40, 42, 43
Under the current owners, this
grungy-chic cellar café/restaurant
on the corner of Nansensgade and
Vendersgade is very popular with
younger locals.

🍴 **STICKS 'N' SUSHI**
Japanese   €€-€€€
☎ 33 16 14 07; www.sushi.dk; Nansensgade 47; ⏱ 11.30am-9.30pm Mon-Wed,
11.30am-10pm Thu-Sat; 2-9.30pm;
🚌 5A, 350S, 14, 40, 42, 43; ♿
The original and still the most
stylish contemporary sushi place
in Copenhagen. There's a takeaway
version of the restaurant a few
doors down, with similar opening
hours. Other branches crop up in
various areas within Copenhagen –
check the website for a comprehensive listing of locations.

Chris Skytte
Composer

Favourite lunch spot The food is always delicious at Sticks 'n' Sushi (opposite) on Nansensgade, which is a really unique street. Other than that, I like to grab a sandwich in one of the places on Halmtorvet (p132). **Best gay venue in the city** I really like Amigobar (Schønbergsgade 4), a cosy place that sometimes has karaoke. There is a good mix of a gay and hetero crowd there. **Best place for a birthday treat** I often celebrate my birthday at Grøften in Tivoli (p92). It's a really *hyggelige* (p154) open-air restaurant – you must have a schnapps and a large Fadøl (beer). It is the real Danish experience! **Recommendation for a short-term visitor** I absolutely recommend taking a tour of Christiania (p42). It's an amazing 'free' place in the middle of the city with nature, artists, shops, restaurants and music places. It's a must-see.

⍩ DRINK

BANKERÅT Bar

☎ 33 93 69 88; www.bankeraat.dk; Ahlefeldtsgade 27-29; ⏱ 9.30am-midnight Mon-Fri, 10.30am-midnight Sat-Sun; 🚌 14, 40, 42, 43

This characterful, cultish café-bar has been part of the Nansensgade scene since before there even was a scene. Check out the porn-adorned loos and the freaky taxidermy by local artist Phillip Jensen.

⍩ BARBARELLAH DJ Bar

☎ 33 32 00 61; www.barbarellah.dk; Nørre Farimagsgade 41; ⏱ 10am-midnight Sun-Tue, to 2am Wed & Thu, to 3am Fri & Sat; Ⓜ Nørreport 🚌 14, 40, 42, 43

The current epicentre of Nørreport's nightlife scene is this corner bar-lounge-restaurant, named after owner Barbara (who also produces the art that hangs on the walls and is for sale, along with the furniture and even the clothes the barmen wear). The food is flame-grilled Parillada-style, the interior

Immerse yourself in the freakish décor of Nørreport's perennial drinking hole, Bankeråt

Mixing it up at Barbarellah

over 50 wines – from Argentina, Spain, France and Italy – by the glass. Intimate but relaxed, and blessedly free of wine snobs, although the barmen are extremely knowledgeable.

🍸 MJ COFFEE *Café*

☎ 33 32 01 05; Gothersgade 26; ⏰ 8am-10pm Mon-Thu, 8am-11pm Fri, 9.30am-11pm Sat, 10.30am-8pm Sun; 🚌 350S

A stalwart of the booming Copenhagen coffee-house scene, MJs serves a superb home-blended cuppa, along with soups and smoothies.

⭐ PLAY

☑ FILMHUSETS CINEMATEK *Cinema*

☎ 33 74 34 12, restaurant 33 74 34 17; www.dfi.dk; Gothersgade 55; ⏰ 10am-10pm Tue- Fri, noon-10pm Sat & Sun; 🚌 350S; ♿

The Danish Film Institute's cutting-edge film centre plays classic Danish and foreign film, mostly in short, themed seasons. There is an excellent cinema bookshop here, as well as the stylish restaurant Sult.

is lit by bewitching psychedelic light projections and DJs play at weekends. Almost unbearably cool.

🍸 BIBENDUM *Wine Bar*

☎ 33 33 07 74; www.vincafeen.dk; Nansensgade 45; ⏰ 4pm-midnight Mon-Sat; Ⓜ & S-train Nørreport 🚌 14, 40, 42, 43

Copenhagen's best wine bar is situated in a cosy, rustic cellar on trendy Nansensgade and serves

>RÅDHUSPLADSEN & TIVOLI

Rådhuspladsen (the City Hall Square), Tivoli and Hovedbanegården (the Central Station) constitute the heart of downtown Copenhagen. At night Rådhuspladsen is illuminated by neon advertising on the buildings that surround it, leading to – perhaps slightly overstated – comparisons with Times Square. That said, this is the main gathering point for the Danes on important occasions, such as New Year's Eve.

As well as the town hall and the main gate of Tivoli, there are a couple of other landmarks to look out for here. Towering over everything in central Copenhagen is the Radisson SAS Royal Hotel, designed in 1960 by Denmark's master builder, Arne Jacobsen. A short walk away on the northern side of Axeltorv are two distinctive buildings, the multicoloured Palads cinema (p97) and Cirkusbygningen (the Circus Building), once a permanent circus venue but which, these days, hosts cheesy 'dinner-and-a-show'-type ventures that are best avoided.

RÅDHUSPLADSEN & TIVOLI

SEE
Dansk Design Center 1 C4
Nationalmuseet 2 C4
Ny Carlsberg Glyptotek .. 3 C4
Rådhuset 4 C3
Tivoli Main Entrance 5 B3

SHOP
Politikens Boghallen 6 B3

EAT
Alberto K 7 B4
Grøften 8 B4
The Paul 9 B4

DRINK
Bjørgs 10 B3
Fox Bar 11 B2
Library Bar 12 B4

PLAY
Koncertsal 13 B4
Mojo 14 C3
Palads Cinema 15 B3
Plænen 16 B4
Pumpehuset 17 B3

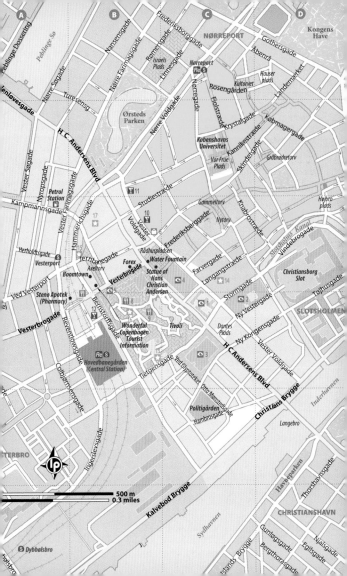

◉ SEE

Danes travel from all over the country to spend the day in Tivoli but Nationalmuseet, Ny Carlsberg Glyptotek and the Dansk Design Center are all major draws here.

◉ DANSK DESIGN CENTER
☎ 33 69 33 69; www.ddc.dk; HC Andersens Blvd 27; adult/concession 50/25kr; 🕙 10am-5pm Mon & Tue, Thu-Fri, 11am-4pm Sat & Sun; 🚇 Central Station 🚌 33; 🚹

Denmark's design museum offers both an imaginative changing exhibition space on the ground floor and a permanent collection of Danish design classics in the

time for each other kr. 30,–

Pills and thrills at the Dansk Design Center

TOP FIVE CHAIRS
The Danes love a good chair, particularly one they've designed themselves. And they have lots to choose from.
> Arne Jacobsen's Egg
> Hans J Wegner's Cow Horn
> Kaare Klint's Safari Chair
> Verner Panton's System 123
> Nanna Ditzel's Wicker Chair

basement. There's a good café and gift shop too.

◉ NATIONALMUSEET
☎ 33 13 44 11; www.natmus.dk; Ny Vestergade 10; admission free; 🕙 10am-5pm Tue-Sun; 🚌 6A, 12, 1A, 2A, 15; 🚹

Denmark's superb national history museum. See also p16.

◉ NY CARLSBERG GLYPTOTEK
☎ 33 41 81 41; www.glyptoteket.dk; Tietgensgade 25; adult/child 50kr/free, Sun free; 🕙 10am-4pm Tue-Sun; 🚇 Central Station 🚌 33, 1A, 2A; 🚹

This exceptional collection of paintings and sculptures, founded by beer baron Carl Jacobsen in 1888, has recently been extensively renovated. The Winter Garden (with a lovely, homely café) that lies at the heart of this vaguely Venetian-looking building has now been returned to its former glory and from here you can meander through a magnificent post-impressionist collection, including a large number of works by Gauguin, and pieces by Cézanne, Van Gogh, Monet and Degas, as well as viewing 5000 years' worth of sculpture.

🕓 RÅDHUSET (TOWN HALL)
☎ 33 66 25 82; www.kbhbase.kk.dk; Rådhuspladsen; admission free for

Rådhus; guided tour of Rådhus 30kr; Verdensur adult/concession 10kr/5kr; tower tour 20kr; 🕓 8.30am-4.30pm Mon-Fri, 10am-1pm Sat; 🚇 Central Station 🚌 10, 12, 14, 26, 29, 33, 67, 68, 69, 2A, 5A, 6A; ♿

This sturdy, national romantic-style town hall is the centre of political power in the city. On

LIKING THE VIKINGS

The Viking empire replaced the Romans as the pre-eminent force in northern Europe for 300 years from the late 8th century. In their state-of-the-art longships, this race of Norsemen – made up of Norwegians, Swedes, Icelanders and Danes – traded and raided as far north as Scotland, west to Ireland and modern-day Canada, east to the Volga river and as far south as North Africa. They colonised much of Ireland and England. The Viking era ended with the arrival of Christianity in the north, around 1066.

The Vikings are famous for their rune stones and horned helmets – the latter in fact misattributed to them (horned helmets were a Bronze Age fashion). They also gave us Bluetooth, or at least the name, which comes from one of their kings, Harold Bluetooth (it's a Danish invention, by the way). If you ask them, the Danes are proud of their Viking ancestors but they tend to keep it low-key. One of the few places you can learn more about them in Copenhagen is Nationalmuseet (opposite) but if you want to see their extraordinary sailing vessels for yourself, we recommend a trip to Roskilde's **Viking Ship Museum** (☎ 46 30 03 00; www.vikingeskibsmuseet.dk; Vindeboder 12; May-Sep adult/concession/under 17s 80/70kr/free, Oct-Apr 50/40kr/free; 🕓 10am-5pm; 🚇 Roskilde, 🚌 603), 25 minutes west of Copenhagen by train.

Towards the end of the Viking era, the narrow end of the Roskilde fjord was deliberately blocked by the locals, who sailed five ships out onto the water and scuttled them with several tons of stones. Latter-day locals had long harboured a hunch that there was something out there, but it wasn't until researchers made a series of dives in the late 1950s that the truth was revealed, and excavations began in 1962 to raise the ancient vessels. The fragments found were reassembled and put on display in a purpose-built museum, overlooking the water, which opened in 1969. In the 1990s nine more ships were discovered during construction work – some from the Middle Ages, but yet more from the Viking era including one 36m in length. Today the harbour here is an excellent day trip, with open-air workshops, a restaurant and, in the summer, trips on the fjord in recreations of Viking ships or on the **MS Sagafjord** (☎ 46 75 64 60; www.sagafjord.dk).

the right as you enter is a unique clock, the Verdensur, designed by the Danish astromechanic Jens Olsen and built in 1955 at a cost of 1,000,000kr. It displays not only the time locally but also things like the solar time, sunrises and sunsets and even the Gregorian calendar. You can also climb the town hall tower for a great view of the city.

TIVOLI

☎ 33 15 10 01; www.tivoli.dk; Vesterbrogade 3; adult/child 3-11/child 0-2 75/40kr/free; Turpas adult/child 2-11 200/150kr; ☽ 11am-11pm Sun-Thu, to 12.30am Fri, to midnight Sat 13 Apr-21 Jun & 20 Aug-23 Sept; 11am-midnight Sun-Thu, to 12.30am Fri & Sat 22 Jun-19 Aug; 11am-10pm Sun-Thu, to 11pm Fri & Sat, 16 Nov-30 Dec; 11am-8pm 23 Dec, closed 24 & 25 Dec; ☒ Central Station ☒ 6A, 26, 5A, 30, 40, 47, 250S; ☒

There are three entrances to Tivoli: the main one on Vesterbrogade, another opposite the main entrance to the Central Station and one on HC Andersens Blvd opposite Ny Carlsberg Glyptotek. You pay both for entrance and then again for whatever rides you choose thereafter (usually around 15kr each), although a *turpas* (tour pass) covers all the rides. There are, however, plenty of free shows, including the Wednesday and Saturday night fireworks and

The spectacle of Tivoli at night

he live band at Plænen (p97) every Friday at 10pm. Please note the opening times and prices listed in this book were for he 2007 season and may vary slightly in the future. Tivoli is also considering annual opening for Halloween, for which dates will also vary – check the website for details. See also p10.

THE FAIRY TALE OF HIS LIFE

For the Danes, Hans Christian Andersen is Shakespeare, Goethe and Dickens rolled into one. That may sound a little excessive for a fairy-tale writer, but Andersen was far more than that. As well as single-handedly revolutionising children's literature (*Alice in Wonderland*, the works of Roald Dahl and even Harry Potter owe him a debt), he wrote novels, plays and several fascinating travel books.

Stories such as *The Little Mermaid*, *The Emperor's New Clothes* and *The Ugly Duckling* have been translated into over 170 languages and are embedded in the global literary consciousness like few others. Even today, over centuries since his birth, their themes are as relevant and universal as ever.

Andersen was born in Odense on 2 April 1805. In three autobiographies – including *The Fairy Tale of My Life* – he mythologised his childhood as poor but idyllic. But the truth was his mother (a washerwoman) and his father (a cobbler) were not married when he was conceived, and his father died when Andersen was 11.

Andersen left for Copenhagen soon after, an uneducated, gauche 14-year-old on a classic fairy-tale mission: to make his fortune in the big city. He tried and failed at various occupations until he eventually found international success with his writing, initially his poems and plays, and then his first volume of short stories.

Andersen lived the rest of his life in the city at various addresses, primarily on Nyhavn (p62) but also in the Hotel d'Angleterre (p148) and, in his youth, in the attic of what is now Magasin du Nord (p118). You can visit the rooms in the department store; they remain preserved much as they would have been when he lived there.

His later success and accompanying wealth were some compensation for what was an otherwise deeply troubled life. Andersen was a neurotic, sexually ambivalent, highly strung hypochondriac – he left a card reading 'I am only apparently dead' beside his bed each night because of a morbid fear of falling into a deep sleep, being taken for dead and buried alive.

It all perhaps goes some way to explaining why he was such a restless nomad to the last. He travelled further than any of his compatriots, most notably in 1840–41 when he journeyed as far as Istanbul and wrote of his experiences in the highly accomplished travelogue *A Poet's Bazaar*.

Andersen died of liver cancer, at a grand age of 70, in 1875. He is buried in Assistens Kirkegård (p66).

SHOP

Rådhuspladsen is not a major shopping destination. There is a small arcade to the left of the main entrance to Tivoli on Vesterbrogade, which has an Irma supermarket and a bakery, HC Andersen Bageri, where you can stock up for a picnic in Tivoli.

POLITIKENS BOGHALLEN
Books

☎ 33 47 25 60; Rådhuspladsen 37;
🕑 10am-7pm Mon-Fri, to 4pm Sat;
🚃 10, 12, 14, 26, 29
This is the city's biggest book store, with a large English language section.

EAT

The area around Rådhuspladsen has its fair share of fast food outlets, but there are several more appealing alternatives on offer.

ALBERTO K *Italian*   €€€€

☎ 33 42 61 61; www.alberto-k.dk;
Radisson SAS Royal Hotel, Level 20,
Hammerischegade 1; 🕑 noon-3pm
Mon-Fri, 6pm-midnight Mon-Sat; S-train
Vesterport or Central Station 🚃 6A, 26,
5A, 30, 40, 47; ♿
The modern Italian cuisine served here is a match for the panoramic view at this 20th-floor hotel restaurant, which is really saying something. The menu blends

Eating out at Rådhuspladsen

ocally sourced game and fish with
talian ingredients – the venison
vith aged balsamic, pimento
nd a roast garlic and potato ter-
ine being a good example. The
estaurant has a well-established,
nternational wine cellar.

GRØFTEN *Danish*   €€

☎ 33 75 06 75; Tivoli; ✆ noon-10pm
ue-Sun; 🚇 Central Station 🚌 6A, 26,
A, 30, 40; ♿

One of Tivoli's more traditional
Danish offerings, housed in its
oldest building and with a menu
hat includes several different
mørrebrød (p17).

THE PAUL
Modern European   €€€€

☎ 33 75 07 75; www.thepaul.dk; Tivoli;
✆ lunch & dinner Apr-Sep; 🚇 Central
tation 🚌 6A, 26, 5A, 30, 40; ♿

ocated in a crescent conservatory
designed by Poul Henningsen, this
Michelin-starred restaurant –
named after its English owner,
Paul Cunningham – is one of the
ity's finest, serving elegant and
efined modern European food.

🍸 DRINK

he bars and pubs opposite
Tivoli and on Strøget are a popular
Saturday night destination for a
young, boozy crowd but there
re a few other, more interesting
places close by.

Every seat is a window seat at Alberto K

BJØRGS *Café-Bar*

☎ 33 14 53 20; www.cafebjorgs.dk;
Vester Voldgade 19; ✆ 9am-midnight
Mon & Tue, 9am-1am Wed & Thu, 9am-
2am Fri, 10am-2am Sat, 10am-midnight
Sun; 🚌 10, 12, 14, 26, 29

This L-shaped café-bar is a good
people-watching venue and is a
popular after-work drinks haunt.
It also serves simple burgers and
salads.

FOX BAR *Bar*

☎ 33 13 30 00; www.hotelfox.dk; Jarm-
ers Plads 3; ✆ 5pm-midnight Thu, 5pm-
2am Fri & Sat; 🚌 5A, 14, 173E, 33; ♿

On weekend evenings the lobby
of the experimental designer hotel
Fox becomes a supersleek design

Pouline Middleton
Managing Director, Crossroads Copenhagen
(www.crossroadscopenhagen.com)

First port of call The Custom House (p61), in the port, has been restored redecorated by Terence Conran. It has a great atmosphere, and houses and three different restaurants. **Best place to eat out** Alberto K (p94) at Royal Hotel is a good restaurant with a splendid view of the city and the p is decked out with classical Danish design. **Best place to check out the la Danish designs** Designer Zoo (p131) on Vesterbrogade is the place to s for new Danish designs. **Best café to wind down in** Barbarellah (p86) about hanging out on retro sofas. It is like being back in my teenage room a good way! **Top tip** Christiania (p42) is always a fabulous place to go.

hangout, with hilariously laid-back seating, psychedelic décor and a less successful restaurant, Fox Kitchen, which offers strenuously molecular food like parsnip ice cream and flavoured foams.

LIBRARY BAR *Bar*
☎ 33 14 92 62; www.profilhotels.com; Copenhagen Plaza; Bernstorffsgade 4; ⏱ 4pm-midnight Mon-Thu, to 2am Fri & Sat; ⓡ Central Station; ⏲ 10, 15, 26, 30, 40, 47; ♿
The Plaza Hotel's small bar mimics a classic London gentleman's club, with leather chairs, an open fire and shelves lined with books.

⭐ PLAY

This is the heart of the city's big-screen and multiplex cinema district but Tivoli and other smaller-scale venues offer some variety.

MOJO *Live Music*
☎ 33 11 64 53; Løngangstræde 21; ⏱ 8pm-5am; admission 40-80kr; ⓡ Central Station ⏲ 6A, 12, 33
One of the city's leading blues venues with live entertainment every night.

PALADS CINEMA *Cinema*
☎ 70 13 12 11; www.biobooking.dk; Axeltorv 9; S-train Vesterport, Central Station ⏲ 5A, 30, 14, 15; ♿

A multiplex, yes, but one with a garish charm and a large number of choices of both Danish and international films (subtitled in Danish).

PUMPEHUSET *Live Music*
☎ 33 93 19 60; www.pumpehuset.dk; Studiestræde 52; admission 100-260kr; S-train Vesterport, Central Station ⏲ 5A, 30, 14, 15
This popular rock/pop venue lies at the western end of Studiestræde. You don't get too many international names playing here; it's more famous for its jamming sessions themed on famous acts.

TIVOLI'S KONCERTSAL & PLÆNEN *Live Music*
☎ 33 15 10 12; www.tivoli.dk; Tivoli, Vesterbrogade 3; ⓡ Central Station ⏲ 6A, 26, 5A, 30, 40; ♿
Copenhagen's largest concert hall attracts major international acts, often of the easy listening/musical theatre strain – Liza Minnelli played here in 2007. Improbably, this historic building also now has Europe's longest saltwater aquarium. Meanwhile, every Friday at 10pm a major Danish or international pop act performs for free at the open-air stage, Plænen.

>SLOTSHOLMEN

Though small, the 'island' of Slotsholmen is home to Folketinget (the Danish parliament; p102), the Kongelige Bibliotek (the Royal Library; p101) and a treasure trove of other, more quirky delights. It is a beguiling place to walk around, with numerous interesting nooks and crannies to explore, not least a beautiful 'hidden' garden. In the dark winter, when the mist descends and the wind howls in off the Øresund Sea, there are few more atmospheric places in which to summon Copenhagen's 1000-year history.

Slotsholmen is ringed on three sides by the moatlike Frederiksholms canal; its fourth side fronts the harbour with Christianshavn opposite. You reach it via one of eight bridges, the most famous of which being Marmorbroen (the Marble Bridge), which leads directly into the rear courtyard of Christiansborg Slot (p100), Denmark's neobaroque parliament building. This is one of the grandest sights in the city as you arrive in what is still the royal stable yard.

SLOTSHOLMEN

● SEE

Børsen 1 D2
Christiansborg Ruins 2 C2
Christiansborg
Slotskirke 3 C1
Dansk Jødisk Museum 4 D3

De Kongelige Stalde
& Kareter 5 B2
Det Kongelige
Bibliotek 6 D3
Folketinget 7 C2
Holmens Kirke 8 D1
Teatermuseet 9 C2

Thorvaldsens
Museum 10 B1
Tøjhusmuseet 11 C3

❙¶ EAT

Søren K 12 D3

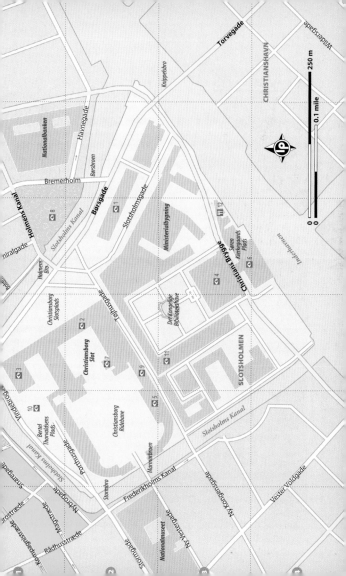

NEIGHBOURHOODS

SLOTSHOLMEN

SEE
BØRSEN

Børsgade; 🚌 1A, 2A, 15, 65E

The former stock exchange's ornate copper spire is made up of four dragons, their tails intertwining as they reach skywards to a height of 50m. It is one of the most striking landmarks in the city. The building still functions as a chamber of commerce but is rarely open to the public.

The twisting tailspin of Børsen's spire

CHRISTIANSBORG RUINS

☎ 33 92 64 92; www.ses.dk; Christiansborg Slot; adult/child 25/10kr; 🕙 10am-4pm; 🚌 1A, 2A, 15, 65E; ♿

In the cryptlike basement museum of Christiansborg you can see the ruins of Bishop Absalon's fortress, dating from 1167.

CHRISTIANSBORG SLOTSKIRKE

Christiansborg Slotsplads; admission free; 🕙 noon-4pm Sun; 🚌 1A, 2A, 15, 65E; ♿

Tragedy struck CF Hansen's dignified neoclassical church (dating from 1826), next-door to the parliament, on the day of the Copenhagen Carnival, 1992. A stray firework hit the scaffolding that had surrounded the church during a lengthy restoration and set the roof ablaze, destroying the dome. Miraculously, a remarkable frieze by Bertel Thorvaldsen that rings the ceiling just below the dome survived. The restorers went back to work and the church was reopened in January 1997.

DANSK JØDISK MUSEUM

☎ 33 11 22 18; www.jewmus.dk; Kongelige Bibiliotekshave (Royal Library garden); adult/concession/child under 16 40/30kr/free; 🕙 1-4pm Tue-Fri, noon-5pm Sat & Sun Sep-May; 🚌 47, 66; ♿

Looking down on the grand Christiansborg Slot

Designed by Polish-born Daniel Libeskind, the Danish Jewish Museum is housed in an early-17th-century building – formerly the Royal Boat House – that has been transformed into an intriguing geometrical space. The museum's entrance is on the southern side of the garden, which lies to the rear of the Kongelige Bibliotek.

🄲 DE KONGELIGE STALDE & KARETER

☎ 33 40 10 10; www.kongehuset.dk; Christiansborg Ridebane 12; adult/child 20/10kr; ⏲ 2-4pm Fri-Sun May-Sep, 2-4pm Sat & Sun Oct-Apr; 🚌 1A, 2A, 15, 65E

The Royal Stables and Coaches Museum has a unique collection of antique coaches, uniforms and riding paraphernalia, some of which is still used for royal occasions.

🄲 DET KONGELIGE BIBLIOTEK

☎ 33 47 47 47; www.kb.dk; Søren Kierkegaards Plads; admission free; ⏲ 9am-9pm Mon-Fri, 9am-5pm Sat; 🚌 47 & 66, Harbour bus; ♿

The Royal Library has two very distinct parts: the original, 19th-century red-brick building and the breathtaking granite-and-glass extension, completed in 1999. The latter, nicknamed the Black Diamond, is the main public draw. People come simply to marvel at the interior with its giant glass wall and views across the harbour, or to enjoy the food in the café or the minimalist Søren K restaurant (p103). You need to be a member to access what is the largest library in Scandinavia, containing 21 million books. Among them are original manuscripts and diaries by Kierkegaard and Hans Christian Andersen (including the fairy-tale writer's unsuccessful application

Granite and glass collide to form the Black Diamond, Det Kongelige Bibliotek

to work at the library). The Black Diamond also hosts popular exhibitions and concerts. Check the website for details. To the rear of the library is Det Kongelige Bibiliotekshave (the Royal Library garden), a pretty, leafy oasis in the heart of the city.

◉ FOLKETINGET

☎ 33 37 55 00; www.folketinget.dk; Rigs-dagsgården; admission free; ⏲ guided tours 2pm Mon-Fri & Sun Jul & Aug, 2pm Sun Sep-Jun; 🚌 1A, 2A, 15, 65E; ♿

The Danish parliamentary chamber is where 179 members of parliament debate national legislation and hold the government to account. Tours in English are given for free in July and August.

◉ HOLMENS KIRKE

☎ 33 13 61 78; www.holmenskirke.dk; Holmens Kanal 9; admission free; ⏲ 9am-2pm Mon-Fri, to noon Sat 🚌 350S

Not actually on Slotsholmen, but just across the canal that rings it to the northeast, the naval church was originally an anchor forge until being converted for worship in 1619. This is where many of Denmark's great seafaring heroes are buried, including Admiral Niels Juel, who defeated the Swedish fleet in the crucial Battle of Køge Bay in 1677. Typical of Lutheran churches, the interior is Spartan, but is notable for its carved, 17th-century oak altarpiece. The Netto Boat canal tours (p178) depart from here also. Dronning

Margrethe and her consort Prince Henri were married here.

☻ TEATERMUSEET

☎ 33 11 51 76; www.teatermuseet.dk; Christiansborg Ridebane 18; adult/concession/child 30/20kr/free; ⏲ 11am-3pm Tue & Thu, 11am-5pm Wed, 1-4pm Sat & Sun; 🚍 1A, 2A, 15, 65E
Lovers of old theatres won't mind that the memorabilia in what used to be the Hofteater (Old Court Theatre) focuses, naturally, on Danish actors and productions. The theatre, which dates (in its current state) back to 1842, closed in 1881 but reopened as a museum in 1922. You can wander backstage, into the dressing rooms, and see the royal box, as well as examine old sets, costumes and posters.

☻ THORVALDSENS MUSEUM

☎ 33 32 15 32; www.thorvaldsens museum.dk; Bertel Thorvaldsens Plads 2; adult/concession/child 20/10kr/free, free Wed, free audioguide; ⏲ 10am-5pm Tue-Sun; 🚍 1A, 2A, 15, 65E ♿
One of the most distinctive buildings in Copenhagen, this colourful Greco-Roman mausoleum with its classically inspired friezes was the country's first purpose-built art museum. It houses the majority of works produced during the long and illustrious career of Bertel Thorvaldsen (1770–1844).

Thorvaldsen spent much of his working life in Rome, where he drew inspiration from classical mythology. The museum contains a fascinating collection of the artist's own collection of art and ancient artefacts from the Mediterranean region...and the artist himself, buried in the main room.

☻ TØJHUSMUSEET

☎ 33 11 60 37; www.thm.dk; Tøjhusgade 3; adult/concession/child 40/20kr/free; ⏲ noon-4pm Tue-Sun; 🚍 1A, 2A, 15, 65E
The Royal Arsenal Museum houses a stunning collection of historic weaponry, from canons and medieval armour to pistols, swords and even a WWII flying bomb. The 163m-long building is Europe's longest vaulted Renaissance hall, built by Christian IV in 1600.

🍴 EAT

🍴 SØREN K
Modern Danish   €€€

☎ 33 47 49 49; www.soerenk.dk; Søren Kierkegaards Plads 1; ⏲ noon-midnight Mon-Sat; 🚍 47 & 66 Harbour Bus; ♿
Bathed in light on even the dourest of days, the sleek, minimalist restaurant of the Black Diamond is one of the most stylish in the city. Its kitchen is dedicated to low-fat, light dishes made from strictly seasonal ingredients.

>STRØGET & AROUND

Strøget is Copenhagen's main pedestrian shopping street (it's actually made up of several streets and squares), said to be the longest of its kind in Europe, and a major gathering point for locals. This is the living heart of the city, made up of a maze of well-preserved, 18th- and 19th-century streets lined with pretty town houses, copper-spired churches and cobbled squares, and usually thronging with a hectic blend of shoppers and cyclists. Cars struggle here as most of the streets around Strøget are either pedestrian or unfathomable one-ways, so it's best to explore the fantastic range of small, independent shops, cosy cafés and stylish restaurants on foot.

STRØGET & AROUND

Please see over for map

SEE

CARITAS SPRINGVANDET

Gammeltorv

The Charity Fountain is the most beautiful in Copenhagen. It was built in 1608 and is a popular rallying point for buskers.

DOMHUSET

Nytorv; 8.30am-3pm Mon-Fri; 6A;

Copenhagen's pink-stucco, neo-classical court house was designed by CF Hansen (also responsible for Vor Frue Kirke, p111) and built in 1815. It is linked by its own 'bridge of sighs' to cells across the road on Slutterigade. The words inscribed above the courthouse steps, 'Med Lov Skal Man Land Bygge' (With Law Shall One Build the Land), are taken from the Jutland Code that codified laws in Denmark in 1241. You can take a peek inside, although they don't encourage casual visitors.

GAMMEL STRAND

6A;

Gammel Strand (Old Beach) fronts the canal that partially encircles the island of Slotsholmen. This

Ninteenth-century houses line the canals of Gammel Strand

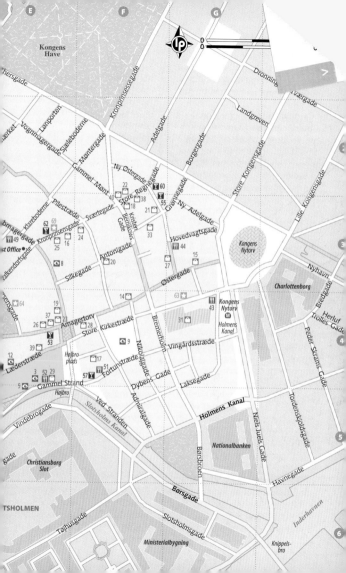

perfectly preserved row of 18th- and 19th-century town houses, with its restaurants and cafés, is among the most picturesque in Copenhagen and a great place for an outdoor drink on a sunny day. This used to be the site of the old fish market, a fact that is commemorated by the statue of the fishwife beside Højbro. On the other side of the bridge, in the waters of the canal itself, you can see a statue of a merman and his children, while facing the fishwife is a grander statue of Bishop Absalon, who founded Copenhagen over 1000 years ago. You can also catch the canal tour boats from here (see p177).

☻ HELLIGÅNDSKIRKEN
☎ 33 15 41 44; Nils Hemmingsensgade 5, Strøget; ⏱ noon-4pm Mon-Fri & services on Sun; 🚌 6A; ♿

The Church of the Holy Spirit, located opposite clothing store H&M, dates from the 15th century and sits on the site of an even older monastery founded in the 13th century. It often hosts secondhand book sales.

☻ KUNSTFORENINGEN
☎ 33 36 02 60; www.kunstforeningen .dk; Gammel Strand 48; adult/concession 40/25kr; ⏱ 11am-5pm Tue-Sun; 🚌 6A

The HQ of Denmark's artists' union showcases local and international artistic talent with changing exhibitions. Across the hall, the Fotografisk Center holds temporary photographic exhibitions by leading Danish and international photographers.

☻ KØBENHAVN UNIVERSITET BIBLIOTEK (COPENHAGEN UNIVERSITY LIBRARY)
☎ 33 47 47 47; Fiolstræde 1; admission free; ⏱ 10am-7pm Mon-Fri; Ⓜ & S-train Nørreport 🚌 6A

The main university building in this part of town faces Vor Frue Kirke (p111) across the higgledy-piggledy cobbles of Vor Frue Plads. In the lobby you can see one of the most curious sights in all of Copenhagen: a British cannonball fired from the fleet that attacked the city in 1807. The cannonball is said to have fallen through the roof of Trinitatiskirke (behind the Rundetårn, p110), where the library used to be kept, and landed in a book, which remains embedded with five metal fragments today. The book's title? *Defensor Pacis* (Defender of Peace).

☻ LATIN QUARTER
🚌 6A; ♿

This small corner of the city centre has little in common with the Latin Quarter of Paris, but gets its nickname from the presence of

CHEER UP, IT'S NOT ALL BAD…

Denmark's most famous philosopher, Søren Kierkegaard, was regarded as 'the father of existentialism'. Born into a prosperous Copenhagen family on 5 May 1813 (in a house on Nytorv where the Danske Bank now stands), he inherited a large fortune and used it to finance his musings on morality and God. Kierkegaard studied theology and philosophy at Copenhagen University but it was his rejection by his one, great love, Regine Olsen, that proved to be the major impetus behind his writing. His first great work, *Either/Or* (1843) examined the conflict between aesthetic pleasures and the ethical life, followed by *Fear and Trembling* and the less catchy *Concluding Unscientific Postscript to the Philosophical Fragments*. One of his earliest works was a complex criticism of his Copenhagen contemporary Hans Christian Andersen. Andersen would be just one of many enemies the cantankerous Kierkegaard would make in a short life that ended in death from exhaustion in 1855.

the university (now home to the law faculty) and the secondhand bookshops and cafés that grew up around it. The Latin Quarter stretches east from Vor Frue Plads along Store Kannikestræde and Skindergade to Købmagergade, via the pretty Gråbrødretorv (Grey Friar's Square, founded in the mid-17th century), with its open-air restaurants and bars, and north up Fiolstræde to Nørre Voldgade. There are several inviting cafés, bars and interesting shops here.

◉ MUSEUM EROTICA

☎ 33 12 03 11; www.museumerotica
.dk; Købmagergade 24; 109kr; ⏰ 10am-11pm May-Sept, 11am-8pm Sun-Thu, 10am-10pm Sat & Sun Oct-Apr

This cross between a peepshow and a museum is probably the least erotic place in town – as well

as its most expensive museum – but there are enjoyably salacious exhibits on the sex-lives of the rich, famous and shameless including Hitler, Marx, Freud, Monroe and the surprisingly well-endowed Toulouse Lautrec. The 'shock room' at the end of the tour had the desired effect on us and is not for those of a sensitive disposition.

◉ NIKOLAJ KIRKE

☎ 33 93 16 26; www.nikolaj-ccac
.dk; Nikolaj Plads 10; adult/concession 20/10kr; opening times vary; Ⓜ Kongens Nytorv ⊞ 350S; ♿

This 13th-century church is now the home of the Copenhagen Contemporary Arts Centre, which hosts around half a dozen exhibitions of contemporary art each year.

NEIGHBOURHOODS

STRØGET & AROUND

Shopaholics of the world unite at Strøget

PISSERENDEN

🚌 6A, 12, 26, 29, 33

This cosy grid of shopping streets lies immediately to the north of Strøget. Its shops are younger and more 'alternative' than the main drag, with clothing stores, secondhand CD shops, cafés, bars and bagel shops. A century or so ago this was a rather unsavoury part of town, full of brothels and *bodegas* (pubs), but these days it is a bustling network of streets (Studiestræde, Larsbjørnstræde and Vestergade are the main

ones), popular with students and creative types from the advertising and design studios nearby.

RUNDETÅRN

☎ 33 73 03 73; www.rundetaarn.dk; Købmagergade 52A; adult/child 20/5kr; 🕐 10am-5pm Mon-Sat Sep-May, 10am-8pm Mon-Sat, noon-5pm Sun Jun-Sep; Observatory 7-10pm Tue & Wed Oct-Mar, 1-4pm Sun Jul-Aug; Ⓜ & S-train Nørreport 🚌 350S

One of the city's most striking landmarks (see also p11).

STRÆDET

🚌 6A; ♿

Running parallel to Strøget to the south is Strædet, perhaps the most beautiful shopping street in the city. It is less grand than Strøget, but Strædet's two streets, Kompagnistræde and Læderstræde, are far more charming and packed with less-mainstream shops. Its strong points are its excellent range of independent jewellers and antique silver shops, but there are several good cafés here too. Though supposedly pedestrian, cars and, more perilously, fast-moving cyclists do still venture this way, so keep your wits about you.

VOR FRUE KIRKE

☎ 33 37 65 40; www.koeben havnsdomkirke.dk; Nørregade 8; admission free; ⏰ 8am-5pm Mon-Sat, noon-5pm Sun; S-train Nørreport 🚌 6A; ♿

Copenhagen's Domkirke (cathedral) is an austere, neoclassical building designed by CF Hansen and dates back to 1829. Crown Prince Frederik married Mary Donaldson here in 2004 amid great celebration. It is worth visiting to see the imposing sculptures of Christ and the 12 apostles by Denmark's great neoclassical sculptor, Bertel Thorvaldsen (see p103).

The interior of the neoclassical Vor Frue Kirke lights up at Christmas time

SHOP

Running through the heart of what must be one of the most charming city centres in Northern Europe are the pedestrian streets that together make up Strøget (pronounced 'stroll'). Strøget begins at Rådhuspladsen with some downmarket clothing stores, pubs and fast-food joints, but picks up the pace when it arrives at the picturesque double-squares of Nytorv and Gammeltorv (Old and New Square). From here the shops move progressively upmarket – although remaining resolutely mainstream – past the Royal Copenhagen stores on Amagertorv, with its famous 'stork fountain', and onwards to Strøget's conclusion at Kongens Nytorv.

We can't help feeling Strøget is starting to lose its way as a must-see shopping destination. International chains are encroaching and the western end is a not-terribly-appealing mix of kebab kiosks and budget clothing chains while to the east are the kind of high-end labels – Hermes, Gucci, Louis Vuitton – you can find in any big city in Europe.

Hunting for the latest fashion and design on the streets of Strøget

However – and it's a big however – if you take a detour off the main drag, down the small side streets, you will find some real retail treasures. On Strædet (p111), in Pisserenden (p110) and within the area bordered by Strøget, Købmagergade, Kronprinsensgade and Gothersgade, there are dozens of small (and some large) independent shops, selling locally designed homewares, jewellery, clothing, ceramics and glassware. The latter area is the centre of Copenhagen's high-end, establishment fashion scene, home to several flagship stores of notable Scandinavian designers, such as Munthe plus Simonsen (p119) and Day Birger Mikkelsen (p116). It's here that you'll find the city's so-called 'fashion street', Kronprinsensgade, although we would argue that places such as Elmegade and Ravnsborggade in Nørrebro are usurping it these days.

Please note that in cases of shops on or close to Strøget, the bus numbers given are those that go closest to the shops in question, but there may still be some walking to do.

☑ **BIRGER CHRISTENSEN** *Fashion*

☎ 33 11 55 55; www.birger-christensen com; Østergade 38, Strøget; 🕑 10am-6pm Mon-Thu, to 7pm Fri, to 4pm Sat; Ⓜ Kongens Nytorv 🚌 15, 19, 26, 1A

The city's pre-eminent upmarket clothing store sells a wide range of Danish and international brands for both men and women, including Prada, Chanel and YSL. Known in Denmark for its furs.

☑ **BODUM** *Homewares*

☎ 33 36 40 80; www.bodum.com; Østergade 10, Strøget; 🕑 10am-6pm Mon-Thu, to 7pm Fri, to 5pm Sat; Ⓜ Kongens Nytorv 🚌 15, 19, 26, 1A; ♿

The Danish brand famous for its simple but elegant coffee-making paraphernalia also sells kitchen- and tableware and storage products at its towering flagship store here at the top of Strøget. The stylish Swedish stationery brand Ordning & Reda – part of the same group and with its own store on nearby Grønnegade – is on the second floor.

☑ **BRUUNS BAZAAR** *Fashion*

☎ 33 32 19 99; www.bruunsbazaar.com; Kronprinsensgade 8 & 9; 🕑 10am-6pm Mon-Thu, to 7pm Fri, to 4pm Sat; 🚌 350S

Bruuns Bazaar is now an internationally recognised fashion label selling archetypal, contemporary Scandinavian style around the world. This is where the men's and women's Bruuns Bazaar stores began – they also stock other well-known brands.

Stine Bülow
Jeweller (see opposite)

Best weekend party venue I often go out with friends to Boutique Lize (p134) in Vesterbro. **Best weekday lunch restaurant** Zirup (p126) on Strædet. **Best for jewellery** My favourite place is Hoff (p117) on Kronprinsensgade, which represents some of the top Danish goldsmiths. **Dream Copenhagen day** For a birthday treat I would take the train to Dyrehaven (p69) to have a picnic and then go to Vega (p136) to dance the night away. **Best place off the tourist track** Copenhagen has so many fantastic small shops that it is hard to pick one. In terms of eating, go for dinner at Spiseloppen (p47) in Christiania. **Don't leave Copenhagen without...** A tour of the canals (p177) is definitely worth doing. **Favourite shop** Tage Andersen, the famous florist on Ny Adelgade. Flowers are a very important thing in life!

☐ BÜLOW *Jewellery*
☎ 66 12 24 04; www.bulowjewellery
.dk; Lille Kirkestræde 5; ⌚ 11am-6pm
Wed-Fri, to 2pm Sat; 🚌 350S

...tine Bülow (opposite) is one
of the city's best independent,
contemporary jewellers. Her
...tudio-shop is tucked away
...ehind Højbro Plads and is thus
...asy to miss if you don't know
...t's there. Her delicate, original
...arrings, rings, necklaces and
...racelets skilfully blend metals
...nd precious stones. The results
...re abstract, sophisticated
...nd often have a rough-edge
...nish.

☐ CASA SHOP
Homewares/Furniture
☎ 33 32 70 41; www.casagroup.com;
Store Regnegade 2; ⌚ 11am-5.30pm
Mon-Thu, 11am-6pm Fri, 10am-3pm Sat;
🚌 350S

One of the major – and most
expensive – furniture and homewares stores in the city, packed
full of modern, international (well,
mostly Italian) brands beloved of
the childless and well-heeled.

☐ CHAPEAUX PETITGAS *Hats*
☎ 33 13 62 70; Købmagergade 5;
⌚ 10am-5.30pm Mon-Fri, 10am-2pm Sat

This timewarp gentlemen's milliners has been here since HC

Cap off a day's shopping at headwear specialists Chapeaux Petitgas

Andersen's time and is perfect for your traditional headwear needs.

🏠 DAY BIRGER MIKKELSEN *Fashion*

☎ 33 45 88 80; www.day.dk; Pilestræde 16; ⏱ 10am-6pm Mon-Thu, to 7pm Fri, to 4pm Sat; 🚌 350S; ♿

The magnificent new flagship store for this leading Danish brand is right in the heart of the mainstream fashion district. Birger's clothes are elegant, classic and sexy, with just a hint of hippy (and that's just the menswear). Designer Malene Birger's own shop (she is no longer part of the Day group) is just around the corner on Antonigade 10 and has the same opening hours.

🏠 FILIPPA K *Fashion*

☎ 33 93 80 00; www.filippa-k.com; Ny Østergade 13; ⏱ 11am-6pm Mon-Thu, to 7pm Fri, to 4pm Sat; 🚌 350S

This is Swedish designer Filippa Kihlborg's flagship Danish store, selling her simple, modern, often monochromatic men's and women's ranges – both day-to-day stuf and more dressy partywear.

🏠 FRYDENDAHL *Homewares/gifts*

☎ 33 13 63 01; www.janfrydendahl.dk; Store Regnegade 1; ⏱ 11am-5.30pm Mon-Thu, to 6pm Fri, to 4pm Sat; 🚌 350S

Jan Frydendahl has been scouring the world for beautiful and quirky

Classic clothing for day or night at Day Birger Mikkelsen

ome design items for 30 years
and his shop sells an eclectic and
ascinating range of products;
everything from chandeliers to
watering cans spills out onto the
pavement in front of his store.

GEORG JENSEN Silver
☎ 33 11 40 80; www.georgjensen.dk;
Amagertorv 4; ⌚ 10am-6pm Mon-Thu,
to 7pm Fri, to 5pm Sat; 🚌 350S; ♿
This is the world famous silver-
smith's flagship store, selling everything from tiepins and watches, to
silverware and gold pieces. It can
be fearfully expensive but popular
gifts for under 200kr include their
iconic elephant bottle openers,
bottle trays and picture frames.

HAY.CPH Homewares/Gifts
☎ 99 42 44 00; www.hay.dk; Pilestræde
29-31; ⌚ 10am-6pm Mon-Thu, 10am-
7pm Fri, 11am-4pm Sat; 🚌 350S
Rolf Hay's fabulous interior design
store sells well-chosen examples
of the latest Danish furniture as
well as wonderful gifts, including
Andreas Lintzer's cuddly towelling
toys, books and homewares. Look
out for their ceramic versions of
plastic vending machine cups.

HOFF Jewellery
☎ 33 15 30 02; Kronprinsensgade 12;
⌚ 11am-5.30pm Tue-Thu, 11am-7pm
Fri, 11am-3pm Sat; 🚌 350S
Ingrid Hoff selects only the best
Danish contemporary art jewellery

Great gift ideas aplenty at Hay.CPH

for her showroom. Though her
designers mix gold and silver with
acrylic and nylon, this is not just
of-the-moment fashion jewellery,
but one-off and limited run pieces
to last a lifetime.

ILLUMS BOLIGHUS
Homewares
☎ 33 14 19 41; www.royalshopping
.com; Amagertorv 8-10, Strøget;
⌚ 10am-6pm Mon-Thu, to 7pm Fri,
to 5pm Sat, noon-5pm first Sun of the
month; 🚌 350S; ♿
If you only have time for one store
in Copenhagen, this might well be
the one. The Bolighus specialises in top-notch contemporary

interior design, clothing, jewellery and furniture from big-name local and international designers. A little further east is its larger, sister department store, Illum.

🏠 KRANSEKAGEHUS Food
☎ 33 13 19 02; Ny Østergade 9; 🕑 10am-6pm Mon-Fri, to 4pm Sat; 🚌 350S

One of the best city-centre bakeries, Kransekagehuset specialises in the traditional marzipan cake known as *kransekage*.

🏠 LE KLINT Homewares
☎ 33 11 66 63; www.leklint.com; Store Kirkestræde 1; 🕑 10am-5.30pm Mon-Thu, to 6pm Fri, to 3pm Sat; 🚌 350S

These stunning handmade, concertina-style lampshades are works of art in themselves. Every Danish home boasts at least one of Klint's classic designs but their newer shades are every bit as interesting and rather more colourful.

🏠 LOUIS POULSEN Homewares
☎ 33 29 86 70; www.louispoulsen.dk; Gammel Strand 28; 🕑 10am-4pm Mon-Fri; 🚌 350S

The new showroom of the famous Danish lighting brand, next to Thorvaldsens Hus (p123) on Gammel Strand, offers state-of-the-art Scandinavian lighting design.

🏠 LUST Erotica
☎ 33 33 01 10; www.lust.dk; Mikkel Bryggers Gade 3A; 🕑 11am-7pm Mon-Thu, to 9pm Fri, to 6pm Sat; 🚌 6A, 12, 29, 33

Lust brings erotica into the mainstream, selling an eye-popping range of sex toys and videos. It is located just off Strøget and a long way – literally and spiritually – from grubby old Istedgade.

🏠 MAGASIN DU NORD Department Store
☎ 33 11 44 33; www.magasin.dk; Kongens Nytorv 13; 🕑 10am-7pm Mon-Thu, to 8pm Fri, to 5pm Sat; Ⓜ Kongens Nytorv 🚌 15, 19, 26, 1A; ♿

The best thing about this slightly old-fashioned but impressive department store – the oldest in Scandinavia, in fact – is its gourmet food hall in the basement. This is also where you will find the city's best range of international magazines.

🏠 MATAS Health & Beauty
☎ 33 32 90 00; www.matas.dk; Amagertorv 24; 🕑 10am-6pm Mon-Fri, to 4pm Sat; 🚌 350S

Matas is a national chain of health and beauty stores (like Boots, but without the dispensing chemists), selling a wide range of vitamins, nonprescription medicines and beauty products. This one, in the heart of Strøget, stocks products

fashion scene in recent years. Naja and Karen started the company in 1994 and have built a global following for their light, shimmering and glamourous (but still practical) clothing, counting the Crown Princess and Helena Christensen among their fans.

NORDISK KORTHANDEL
Books
☎ 33 38 26 38; Studiestræde 26;
🕑 10.30am-5.30pm Mon-Fri, 9.30am-3pm Sat; 🚌 10, 12, 14, 26, 29, 33
The best shop in the city for travel books and maps, mostly in English.

PETER BEIER *Food*
☎ 33 93 07 17; www.peterbeierchoko lade.dk; Skoubogade 1; 🕑 10am-6pm Mon-Thu, to 7pm Fri, to 4pm Sat;
🚌 6A; 🚾
The doyen of Copenhagen's booming artisanal chocolatier scene. Small, but filled with handmade chocolate treats.

ROSENTHAL STUDIO-HAUS
Homewares
☎ 33 14 21 01; www.rosenthal.dk; Fre deriksberggade 21, Strøget; 🕑 10am-6pm Mon-Thu, to 7pm Fri, to 5pm Sat;
🚌 10, 12, 14, 26, 29, 33; 🚾
This high-end design store majors in French and Scandinavian glassware and kitchenware including Global knives, Versace tableware,

Need a magazine? Stop at Magasin du Nord

by the Danish skin-care guru, Ole Henriksen.

MUNTHE PLUS SIMONSEN
Fashion
☎ 33 32 03 12; www.muntheplus simonsen.dk; Grønnegade 10; 🕑 10am-6pm Mon-Thu, to 7pm Fri, to 5pm Sat;
🚌 350S; 🚾
This lavish shop is the main showroom for one of the leading women's fashion brands to emerge from the vibrant Danish

Georg Jensen silverware and bits and pieces from Philippe Starck.

🏠 ROYAL COPENHAGEN PORCELAIN *Homewares*

☎ 33 13 71 81; www.royalshopping.com; Amagertorv 6, Strøget; ⏱ 10am-6pm Mon-Thu, to 7pm Fri, to 5pm Sat, noon-5pm 1st Sun of the month; 🚌 350S; ♿

This is the main showroom for the historic Royal Danish Porcelain, one of the most popular souvenirs to take from a visit to the city since Nelson's time (legend has it he took some home after bombarding the city in 1807). Its 'blue fluted' pattern is famous around the world, as is its Flora Danica dinner service, costing upwards of a million kroner for a full set. The shop was recently refurbished and is definitely worth visiting even if you have no intention of buying anything.

🏠 RÜTZOU *Fashion*

☎ 33 32 63 20; www.rutzou.com; Store Regnegade 3; ⏱ 11am-5pm Mon-Thu, to 6pm Fri, to 4pm Sat; 🚌 350S

One of the leading names in contemporary Danish fashion, Susanne Rützou now has this impressive store in the city's fashion quarter. If you are searching for that kooky-feminine Copenhagen look, this is where you'll find it.

Ceramic and glass items on display at Stilleben

🏠 STILLEBEN *Ceramics*

☎ 33 91 11 31; www.stilleben.dk; Læderstræde 14, Strædet; ⏱ 11am-6pm Mon-Thu, to 7pm Fri, to 4pm Sat; 🚌 6A

This tiny boutique is a favourite on the pedestrian street Strædet. Owners Ditte and Jelena are graduates of the Danish Design School's ceramic and glass course, and stock a contemporary and stunningly beautiful range of ceramic and glass from young, local designers.

🏠 STORM *Fashion*

☎ 33 93 00 14; Store Regnegade 1; ⏱ 11am-5.30pm Mon-Thu, 11am-7pm Fri, 10am-4pm Sat; 🚌 360S

Having recently graduated from the fashion 'underground' on Elmegade, this Danish fashion house now has a large corner store in the heartland of the city's fashion establishment. Storm sells an imprerssive range of Danish and international labels including Chloé, Dior, Burberry and Anne Demeulemeester, as well as design books, CDs and fashion magazines.

◻ SØSTRENE GRENE
Homewares/Food

www.grenes.dk; Amagertorv 29; ⊙ 10am-6pm Mon-Thu, to 7pm Fri, to 5pm Sat; 🚌 350S

Few emerge from Søstrene Grene's warren-like aisles of trashy/cheap/neat-stuff-to-buy without at least a couple things they never knew they needed (dog bowls, a bag of tea, some marbles, scented candles) but would never find cheaper anywhere else.

⊞ EAT

⊞ AURA *Mediterranean* €€

☎ 33 36 50 60; www.aura.dk; Rådhusstræde 4; ⊙ 6pm-midnight Tue-Thu, to 3am Fri & Sun; 🚌 6A

This stylish, modern restaurant/DJ bar serves tapas-sized servings of sparklingly creative modern Mediterranean cuisine. Good value for money and a cool place to boot.

⊞ CAFÉ A PORTA *French* €€

☎ 33 11 05 00; www.cafeaporta.dk; Kongens Nytorv 17; ⊙ 11am-midnight Mon-Thu, 11am-1am Fri, 10am-1am Sat, 10am-6pm Sun; Ⓜ Kongens Nytorv 🚌 15, 19, 26, 1A

Right by the metro station and next door to Magasin du Nord (p118), this magnificent Viennese café used to be a favourite of HC Andersen's. It serves excellent, sizeable portions of classic brasserie food.

A MATTER OF TASTE

The Danes' usually unimpeachable good taste reveals its 'quirkier' side in some of their most popular foodstuffs.

> Pickled herring in curry sauce – Is this the most disturbing food combination ever?
> Salt liquorice – Do you eat it or leave it out for the slugs?
> *Remoulade* – A tart, celery-based mayonnaise. The Danes dollop it on everything, given half a chance.
> *Stegt flæsk med persille sovs* – A dish of pork fat, and nothing else, in parsley sauce. Mmmm.
> *Peberod* – Or 'horseradish', which the Danes cook to accompany meat, fish and everything else.

☗ CAFÉ VICTOR
French €€–€€€

☎ 33 13 36 13; www.cafevictor.dk; Ny Østergade 8; ✿ 8am-1am Mon-Wed, 8am-2am Thu-Sat; 11am-11pm Sun; 🚌 350S

This classic French bar and brasserie is the doyen of the Copenhagen café scene and is enjoyably snobbish with jet-set pretensions and, generally, a more middle-aged crowd (regulation uniform: loafers, jeans and blazers for the men, Chanel for the women). The food is excellent, but a touch overpriced.

☗ HUSET MED DET GRØNNE TRÆ *Danish* €

☎ 33 12 87 86; www.husetmed-detgroennetrae.dk; Gammel Torv 20; ✿ 11.30am-3.30pm Mon-Fri, noon-4pm Sat; 🚌 6A

The 'green tree' of the title was cut down some years before (and replaced with a public toilet), but this cosy cellar restaurant maintains much of its charm with a lengthy menu of smørrebrød – from 39kr and with a wide range of herring toppings – and traditional lunch staples.

☗ LA GLACE *Café* €

☎ 33 14 46 46; Skoubougade 3-5; ✿ 8.30am-5.30pm Mon-Thu, 8.30am-6pm Fri, 9am-5pm Sat; 11am-5pm Sun; 🚌 6A

This enchanting cake and coffee shop next door to Peter

Beier (p119) dates back to 1879. It serves some diet-busting sponge-mousse-cream concoctions, and the best hot chocolate in town.

☗ PEDER OXE
Danish/Global €€

☎ 33 11 00 77; Gråbrødretorv 11; ✿ 11.30am-1am; Ⓜ & S-train Nørreport 🚌 6A

This terrific all-organic restaurant is a stalwart of the city's dining scene

Have an organic experience at Peder Oxe

and serves modern European and Danish food amid a beautiful interior with wooden floors and Portuguese tiles. Downstairs is one of the city's few wine bars.

🍴 PETIT DELICÉ
Danish/Global €€

☎ 33 32 30 48; Kompagnistræde 2, Strædet; 🕙 10am-midnight Mon-Sat; 🚌 6A

This cellar café-restaurant on Strædet had just opened when we visited but it is one of the cosiest places in town, with a lovely open fire as you enter and an engaging menu including locally caught seafood, foraged ingredients (nettles, wild flowers, fresh beech shoots in spring), and a lavish champagne brunch for 169kr.

🍴 POST & TELE MUSEUM CAFÉ *Danish* €-€€

☎ 33 41 09 86; www.cafehovedtele grafen.dk; Købmagergade 37; 🕙 10am-5pm Tue & Thu-Sun, 10am-8pm Wed, 11am-3pm Sun; Ⓜ & S-train Nørreport; ♿

This modern space does its best to bring the not overtly fascinating story of Post Danmark to life. The chief draw, however, is the excellent rooftop café, which serves a reasonable Danish-style lunch and has an outdoor terrace with fantastic views across the city centre to Christiansborg.

🍴 RIZRAZ *Mediterranean* €

☎ 33 15 05 75; www.rizraz.dk; Kompagnistræde 20; 🕙 11.30am-midnight; 🚌 6A

A super-quality, bargain, southern Mediterranean buffet is the main draw in this eternally popular budget restaurant (with another branch at Store Kannikstræde). There's plenty of outdoor seating in summer.

🍴 SLOTSKÆLDEREN HOS GITTE KIK
Danish €

☎ 33 11 15 37; Fortunstræde 4; 11am-3pm Tue-Fri; 🚌 350S

This lunchtime smørrebrød restaurant is full of atmosphere and traditional Danish charm. Just point to the sandwich you want, and Gitte will prepare it and send it to your table.

🍴 THORVALDSENS HUS
Danish €€ –€€€

☎ 33 32 04 00; www.thorvaldenshus .dk; Gammel Strand 34; 🕙 11am-10pm Mon-Thu & Sun, 11am-midnight Fri & Sat; 🚌 1A, 2A, 15, 65E

This stylish restaurant-café-bar has views to Christiansborg Slotskirke and offers a sumptuous menu of Franco-Danish food, such as grilled scallops with cauliflower puree and foie gras with shallot marmalade and winter truffle.

Enter Café Europa to sample some of Copenhagen's best coffee

Y DRINK

Y CAFÉ EUROPA Café

☎ 33 14 28 89; Amagertorv 1, Strøget;
⏱ 8am-midnight Mon-Fri, 9am-2am
Sat, 9am-11pm Sun

Martin Hildebrandt, who runs
this popular meeting place in the
heart of the busy shopping area
of Strøget, has won awards for
his coffee, which he makes from
his own special blend of home-
roasted beans. This is one of the
best places to watch Copenhagen
go by, especially in summer when
there is outdoor seating beside
the elegant Storkspringvandet
(stork fountain).

Y CAFÉ STELLING Café

☎ 33 32 93 00; Gammeltorv 6;
⏱ 9am-11pm Mon-Thu, to 2am Fri &
Sat; 🚌 6A

Designed by Arne Jacobsen, this
light, airy corner café is tucked
away in the northern side of the
old square. Jacobsen's austere
design contrasts with the monu-
mental, Florentine palace-style
bank next door and, completing
what is one of the most extraordinary architectural ensembles in

town, a late-Renaissance Chinese restaurant on the corner.

☗ GRILL BAR *DJ Bar/Lounge*
☎ 33 14 34 54; Ny Østergade 14;
🕐 9am-1am Mon-Sat; 🚌 350S
Horrendously expensive it may be (over 100kr for a cocktail?), but that's the price you pay to spend an evening among Copenhagen's beautiful people in this gorgeous two-storey lounge bar owned by the people behind the former restaurant/bar Konrad. There's a DJ on weekends and reasonable contemporary international food is served throughout the day and evening.

☗ JAILHOUSE *Gay*
☎ 33 15 22 55; www.jailhousecph .dk; Studiestræde 12; 🕐 bar 2pm-2am Sun-Thu, 2pm-5am Fri & Sat, restaurant Thu-Sat 6-10pm; 🚌 5A, 14, 173E, 6A
This two-storey, jail-themed restaurant-bar is one of the most popular venues on the Copenhagen gay scene.

☗ K-BAR *Cocktail Bar*
☎ 33 91 92 22; www.k-bar.dk; Ved Stranden 20; 🕐 3pm-1am Mon-Thur, 3pm-2am Fri, 5pm-2am Sat; 🚌 350S
This laid-back lounge–cocktail bar is tucked away behind Amager-torv. The 'K' stands for Kirsten, who mixes a mean Mojito to a youngish, weekend-all-week and preclub crowd.

☗ SPORVEJEN *Café/Bar*
☎ 33 13 31 01; Gråbrødretorv 17;
🕐 11am-midnight; Ⓜ & S-train Nørreport 🚌 6A
This tram-in-the-wall bar is rather tight on space (it is, literally, one of the old trams that used to run in the city), but has plenty of outdoor seating when weather permits. Great for a beer, not a bite.

☗ STUDENTERHUSET *Bar*
☎ 35 32 38 61; www.studenterhuset .ku.dk; Købmagergade 52; 🕐 noon-6pm Mon, to midnight Tue & Sun, to 1am Wed, to 2am Thu & Fri, to around 4am Sat; 🚌 350S
The student bar of the local university residential building is open to all with keen drink prices and usually something happening every night (and admission is usually free), be it a quiz or live music.

☗ ZEZE *Bar*
☎ 33 14 23 90; www.zeze.dk; Ny Øster-gade 20; 🕐 8am-midnight Mon-Thu, to 2am Fri, 9am-2am Sat; 🚌 350S
Right in the heart of the city centre nightlife scene is this popular café-restaurant-bar that lures the young and the beautiful to an evening of simple, modern Mediterranean cooking and a more relaxed vibe than Grill (left) next door.

Zirup is ideal for a snack or a drink

☎ ZIRUP *Café*

☎ 33 91 31 51; www.azhiba.dk; Læderstræde 32, Strædet; 🕙 10am-1am Mon-Thu, to 2am Fri-Sat; 🚌 6A; ♿

This is one of the best café-restaurants on Strædet with a fresh and funky menu (burgers, Mexican, wraps, sandwiches and salads) to match its colourful, cosmopolitan interior design, but is also a great drinking spot when the sun goes down. There is plenty of outdoor seating during the summer – perfect to see and be seen.

☎ ZOO BAR *DJ Bar*

☎ 33 15 68 69; www.zoobar.dk; Kronprinsensgade 7; 🕙 11am-11pm Mon-Wed, to 2am Thu-Sat; 🚌 350S

It doesn't look like much by day, but this small bar on the so-called 'fashion street' heaves with a young crowd when the DJs hit the decks at weekends.

⭐ PLAY

⭐ CLUB EMMA *Club*

☎ 33 11 20 20; www.emma.dk; Lille Kongensgade 16; 🕙 11pm-5am Thu-Sat; admission Thu/Fri/Sat 60/70/80kr; Ⓜ Kongens Nytorv 🚌 15, 19, 26, 1A

One of the city's largest nightclubs is housed in a 19th-century town house beside Magasin du Nord (p118). There is a lounge-cocktail bar, open-air terrace (the only place you are allowed to smoke) and several dance floors with live music and DJs. The entry age goes from 18 on Thursdays to 19 on Fridays and 22 on Saturdays.

⭐ COPENHAGEN JAZZHOUSE *Live Music*

☎ 33 15 26 00; www.jazzhouse.dk; Niels Hemmingsensgade 10; 🕙 6pm-midnight Sun-Thu, 6pm-5am Fri & Sat; 🚌 6A, 350S

In just about any other city a venue as great as this would be horribly commercialised but Copenhagen's premiere jazz venue has a wonderfully unpretentious atmosphere that focusses on the music and performers. As well as some of the top names in the jazz world, you'll hear funk, blues, pop and, when the DJs get the downstairs dance floor heaving, an even wider range of contemporary music.

⭐ GRAND TEATRET *Cinema*
☎ 33 15 16 11; www.grandteatret.dk; Mikkel Bryggersgade 8; ⓡ Central Station, 🚌 6A, 26, 5A, 30, 40
This attractive cinema, just off Strøget and close to Rådhuspladsen, is good for international arthouse movies.

⭐ HUSET *Club/Bar/Cinema/Restaurant*
☎ 33 15 20 02; www.husetmagstraede.dk; Rådhusstræde 13; admission and opening times vary; 🚌 6A; ♿
This excellent arts centre is home to a variety of entertainments: Musik Cafeen, which promotes up-and-coming pop and rock acts and is a nightclub at the weekends; Salon K, home to improv, experimental theatre and cabaret; the gay nightclub Boiz; a small arthouse movie cinema; and 1.Sal, a live jazz and world-music venue. Oh, and there's a café too. Use it

(p179), the young person's information centre, is also based here.

⭐ LA FONTAINE *Jazz*
☎ 33 11 60 98; www.lafontaine.dk; Kompagnistræde 11, Strædet; 🕐 8pm-5am, live music 11pm-3am Fri & Sat, 9pm-1am Sun; admission varies; 🚌 6A
Copenhagen's oldest and cosiest jazz venue is right in the city centre. It offers live jazz from Friday to Sunday and is renowned for its late-night jam sessions.

⭐ PAN DISCO *Gay*
☎ 33 11 37 84; www.pan-kbh.dk; Knabrostræde 3; 🕐 10pm-6am Fri & Sat; ⓡ Central Station, 🚌 6A
This is Denmark's largest gay club but allcomers – so to speak – are welcome and a fun time is guaranteed.

⭐ PLEX MUSIK TEATER *Theatre/Art*
☎ 33 32 38 30, tickets 33 32 55 56; www.plex-musikteater.dk; Kronprinsensgade 7; admission and opening times vary; 🚌 350S
Copenhagen's new avante-garde music and arts venue hosts a wide range of artistic crossover performances, exhibitions, hybrid art and talks.

>VESTERBRO & FREDERIKSBERG

Vesterbro was once a working-class area known for its butchers and prostitutes. In the late 1990s its proximity to the city centre began to draw in the artsy crowd, followed by the young professionals and, predictably, housing prices skyrocketed. Now it has some of the city's coolest restaurants, cafés, shops and nightlife. It fans out in a westerly direction from the city's Central Station.

Leafy, stately Frederiksberg begins further west at Frederiksberg Allé. This broad, tree-lined avenue is lined with *fin de siécle* apartment blocks – some of the most desirable in the city. It finishes at Frederiksberg Have (p130), the city's most romantic park, with a boating lake, rolling lawns and, looking down from the hill, Frederiksberg Slot and Copenhagen Zoo (p131). Ten minutes or so south of here – in Valby – is the world famous Carlsberg Brewery (p130) with its free museum and visitors centre.

VESTERBRO & FREDRIKSBERG

◉ SEE
Carlsberg Visitors
Center.................................1 B4
Frederiksberg Have........2 B3
Københavns Bymuseet ..3 D3
Zoologisk Have................4 A3
Øksnehallen.....................5 D3

⬜ SHOP
Designer Zoo 6 C3
Granola Food....................7 D3

🍴 EAT
Apropos..............................8 D3
Cofoco................................9 D3
Famo.................................10 D3
Lê Lê Nhà Hàng 11 D3
Les Trois Cochons 12 D3

📺 DRINK
Bang og Jensen 13 C4
Boutique Lize 14 C4
Ricco's Coffee Bar........15 D3

⭐ PLAY
DGI-Byen........................16 D4
Forum..............................17 D2
Imax Tycho Brahe
Planetarium 18 D3
Radiohusets
Koncertsal 19 D2
Vega 20 C4

SEE

CARLSBERG VISITOR CENTRE

☎ 33 27 12 82; www.carlsberg.com; Gamle Carlsberg Vej 11, Valby; adult/concession 40/25kr; ⏰ 10am-4pm Tue-Sun; 🚌 18 & 26; ♿

Carlsberg is one of the largest breweries in the world. It was founded by Christian Jacobsen in 1801 but when Christian's son, Jacob, moved it to the borders of Valby and Frederiksberg in 1847 he renamed the brewery after his son Carl (Carlsberg means 'Carl's Hill'). Soon the company was producing over a million bottles a year, and donating millions of kroner to museums and foundations in Denmark. The recently renovated Carlsberg Visitor Centre offers an entertaining journey through the beer-making process and the story of Carlsberg's global success, with a beer or two at the end included in the price.

Bottled up at the Carlsberg Visitor Centre

FREDERIKSBERG HAVE

Main entrance Frederiksberg Runddel; 🚌 18 & 26; ♿

This is Copenhagen's most romantic park, with lakes, woodlands and lovely picnic lawns. Overlooking it all is Frederiksberg Slot, a former royal palace, now home to the Royal Danish Military Academy and not generally open to the public.

KØBENHAVNS BYMUSEET

☎ 33 21 07 72; www.kbhbymuseum .dk; Vesterbrogade 59, Vesterbro; adult/concession/child 20/10kr/free; ⏰ 10am-4pm Mon & Thu-Sun, to 9pm Wed; 🚌 6A & 26

The city museum is looking a little old-fashioned these days but if you want to find out how Copenhageners used to live, this 18th-century former palace is the place to come.

URBAN STROLL

Istedgade is one of the most charismatic and surprising streets in Copenhagen. The Central Station end is home to the city's infamous sex industry, with shop window displays that would make a Dutchman blush. The junkies and hookers still linger here but persevere a little further and you will find the numerous quirky shops, cafés and bars that have helped transform Vesterbro into one of the city's hippest quarters in recent years. Take a detour left into Halmtorvet (the flagship public project of this recent regeneration), bustling with outdoor restaurants and cafés in spring and summer, and Øksnehallen (below) just across the way.

ZOOLOGISK HAVE

☎ 72 20 02 00; www.zoo.dk; Roskilde-ej 32, Frederiksberg; adult/child 20/60kr; ⏰ 9am-4pm Mon-Fri, to pm Sat & Sun Mar, to 5pm Mon-Fri, to pm Sat & Sun Apr & May, to 9.30pm ul & Aug, to 5pm Mon-Fri, to 6pm Sat Sun Sep, to 5pm Oct, to 4pm Nov-Feb; 🚌 6A; ♿

he new giraffe house is a major ttraction in the city's impressive oo, but 2007 sees the opening of state-of-the-art elephant house esigned by British architect Sir Norman Foster.

ØKSNEHALLEN

☎ 33 86 04 00; Halmtorvet 11, Vest-rbro; www.oeksnehallen.dk; S-train entral Station 🚌 1A, 65; ♿

his former cattle market is now ne of the city's largest and most vely exhibition venues, hosting verything from photographic xhibitions to Copenhagen Cook-ng (p28).

🛍 SHOP

As well as being home to Copenhagen's porn industry and an improbable number of cheap men's hairdressers, Istedgade has some of the most interesting fashion boutiques in the city.

DESIGNER ZOO
Homewares

☎ 33 24 94 93; www.dzoo.dk; Vest-erbrogade 137, Vesterbro; ⏰ 10am-5.30pm Mon-Thur, to 7pm Fri, to 3pm Sat; 🚌 6A & 26

Denmark's renowned design mojo finds its contemporary home at this supercool interior and fashion complex at the unfashionable end of Vesterbro-gade. Here, fashion and furniture designers, as well as ceramic artists and glass blowers, work and sell their highly desirable, limited-edition creations.

NEIGHBOURHOODS

VESTERBRO & FREDRIKSBERG

Seek out the shakes at Granola

🏠 GRANOLA *Food*

☎ 33 25 00 80; Værndemsvej 4, Vesterbro; 🕐 9am-5.30pm Mon-Fri, to 4pm Sat; 🚍 6A, 26, 14, 15

It is easy to miss this wonderfully atmospheric, retro ice-cream and coffee bar in a secluded square, down a short alleyway just off Værndemsvej, but it is worth coming all this way just for their shakes and juice drinks. And don't get us started on the ice cream...

🍴 EAT

🍴 APROPOS

Global   €€ –€€€

☎ 33 23 12 21; www.cafeapropos.dk; Halmtorvet 12, Vesterbro; 🕐 10am-mid-

night Mon-Thu & Sun, to 1am Fri & Sat; S-train Central Station, 🚍 10; 🚻

One of the leading lights of this rejuvenated café square, Apropos serves a free-roaming menu that includes lobster rolls, Tandoori salmon and New York cheesecake with plenty of outdoor seating during summer.

🍴 COFOCO *French*   €

☎ 33 13 60 60; www.cofoco.dk; Abel Cathrines Gade 7, Vesterbro; 🕐 5.30pm-midnight Mon-Sat; 🚍 6A, 26, 10

If Copenhagen Food Consulting merely offered a superb three-course menu, featuring such delights as pork tenderloin with pork cheeks, parsnip and apricots or veal braised in red wine with celery and wild mushrooms, for just 250kr – well, that alone would warrant it a high ranking on the list of the city's best restaurants. But this is a stylish and convivial place too, with diners eating on a giant, communal wooden table beneath sparkling chandeliers. The same owners run the excellent Les Trois Cochons (opposite) and Auberge (p70) in Østerbro.

🍴 FAMO *Italian*   €

☎ 33 23 22 50; Saxogade 3, Vesterbro; 🕐 lunch and dinner Mon-Fri; dinner on Sat & Sun; 🚍 6A, 26

This authentic Italian is usually crowded to the gunwales with enthusiastic foodie locals enjoying a fixed menu that might include wild mushroom risotto, squash puree and long-cooked tomato sauces with fresh, homemade pastas.

LÊ LÊ NHÀ HÀNG
Vietnamese €

☎ 33 22 71 35; Vesterbrogade 56, Vesterbro; ☽ 4-10.30pm Mon, Wed-Sun; 🚌 6A, 26; ⛽

This cavernous, New York–style Vietnamese restaurant on bustling Vesterbrogade is regularly voted the best 'cheap eat' in the Danish press and recently moved to these larger premises with open kitchen and spacious, high-ceilinged din-

ing room. Deep, welcoming bowls of soups, noodles and refined Vietnamese street food will see you stuffed and satiated for under 100kr. If you venture further up Vesterbrogade (to No 56) you will find the original premises, now the Lê Lê Caf, serving excellent Vietnamese-French bistro fare.

LES TROIS COCHONS
French €€

☎ 33 31 70 55; www.cofoco.dk; Værndemsvej 10, Vesterbro; ☽ lunch Mon-Sat, dinner daily; 🚌 6A, 26, 14, 15

This small but glamorous modern French bistro on the so-called 'food street' heaves with a

WORTH A TRIP
Arken (☎ 43 54 02 22; www.arken.dk; Skovvej 100, Ishøj; adult/child 50/35kr; ☽ 10am-5pm Tue & Thu-Sun, to 9pm Wed) was built to mark Copenhagen's stint as European City of Culture in 1996. This remarkable contemporary art museum is as famed for the building that houses it – its nautical ship-shape inspired by its beachfront location on Ishøj Strand – as the international art contained within. After a few years in the doldrums, Arken is bouncing back with a new extension due to open in January 2008 (we recommend you hold off a visit until then, as the museum is not operating at full strength right now). The permanent collection of works created after 1990 includes stunning pieces by top Danish artists of the moment, but equally fascinating is the changing programme of temporary exhibitions that can focus on photography, art or sculpture. The museum has a book store and a wonderful café that hangs, as if it were the ship's lifeboat, on the side of the building – the views across Køge Bay are extraordinary. It is a great place to come with kids as there is plenty of sandy beach space to let off steam after pondering the meaning of Jeff Koon's gigantic flower balloon sculpture. Ishøj Strand is 25 minutes south of Copenhagen. To get to Arden by car, take the E20 motorway and leave at junction 26, following signs for Ishøj Strand. S-trains (lines A or E) leave Copenhagen Central Station twice an hour. From Ishøj station take bus 128, which goes directly to the museum.

DINE WITH THE DANES

If you find yourself travelling to Copenhagen alone, or even with others for that matter, a great way to enjoy some local company is to get in touch with **Dine with the Danes** (☎ 26 85 39 61; www.dinewiththedanes.dk). Originally started by the tourist board in the 1970s, Dine with the Danes restarted as a private operation in 1998 — with some of the original hosts still going strong — offering dinners in the homes of local people. The dinners (adult/child over 7/child 0-7 380/180kr/free) consist of two to three courses, coffee and pastries. Fill in the online request form a week or so in advance and the group will do its best to match you up with an appropriate host (there are gay families available too). More importantly, you'll get to learn more about Denmark and Danish culture straight from the horse's mouth.

bubbling mix of diners every night of the week. Its fixed evening menu (starter, main and dessert) for 250kr has to be one of the city's great dining bargains.

![Y] DRINK

![Y] BANG OG JENSEN
Café/Bar

🕑 33 25 53 18; www.bangogjensen .dk; Istedgade 130, Vesterbro; 🕑 8am-2am Mon-Fri, 10am-2am Sat, 10am-midnight Sun; 🚌 10

This was one of the pioneers during Vesterbro's regeneration days, bringing a young party crowd to what was then the unfashionable end of Istedgade. Appealingly squashy sofas invite you to waste the afternoon here among the crowd of dudes and DJs in this grungy but adorable venue.

![Y] BOUTIQUE LIZE *Bar*

🕑 33 31 15 60; Enghave Plads 6, Vesterbro; 🕑 9pm-1am Wed, 8pm-3am Thu, 8pm-4am Fri & Sat; 🚌 10

This used to be a clothing store but when it was transformed into this Spartan but popular cocktail bar a couple of years back, it just seemed easier to keep the old name. A short walk from Vega (p136), Lize has some of the cheapest cocktails in town and is packed at the weekends. Vesterbro's answer to the Oak Room (p73).

![Y] RICCO'S COFFEE BAR *Coffee*

☎ 33 31 04 40; www.riccos.dk; Istedgade 119, Vesterbro; 🕑 9am-11pm Mon-Fri; 10am-11pm Sat & Sun; 🚌 10

Vesterbro's groovy locals love this tiny but dedicated coffee bar which also sells 20 different types of beans and syrups to take home. Considered by many to be the best coffee bar in Copenhagen.

Dorte Juul
Girl about town

Best place to meet friends for a drink Boutique Lize (opposite), the cocktail bar on Enghave Plads. **Best for a birthday treat** Malbeck (www .malbeck.dk), the Argentinian wine bar on Istedgade. **Best on a sunny day** Halmtorvet in summertime is wonderful, with loads of life. All the cafés, ethnic shops and restaurants, everyone sitting outside until late in the evening – it's just like Southern Europe. Well, almost. **Don't leave Copenhagen without...** Walking along Istedgade from one end to the other – all of human life is here! **Favourite shop** Donn Ya Doll (www.donnyadoll.dk), the women's clothes boutique on Istedgade.

⭐ PLAY

⭐ DGI-BYEN *Sports*
☎ 33 29 80 00; www.dgibyen.dk;
Tietgensgade 65; 🚉 **Central Station**
🚌 **1A & 65E;** ♿

Just south of the Central Station, overlooking the tracks, is Copenhagen's best leisure and sports complex featuring a large indoor swimming pool, bowling alley, spa, restaurant, café and hotel, among other facilities. On offer at the spa are a wide range of beauty treatments, different massage therapies, algae and salt baths, mud packs and acupuncture.

⭐ FORUM *Live Music*
☎ 32 47 20 00; www.forum.dk; **Julius Thomsensplads, Frederiksberg;** Ⓜ **Forum** 🚌 **2A;** ♿

This is one of the city's major concert venues – Bob Dylan and Metallica have performed here in recent years.

⭐ IMAX TYCHO BRAHE PLANETARIUM *Cinema*
☎ 33 12 12 24; www.tycho.dk; **Gammel Kongevej 10, Vesterbro; adult/child 3-12yrs 105/75kr;** 🕑 **9.30am-9pm Mon-Fri, 10.30am-9pm Sat & Sun; S-train Vesterport** 🚌 **14 & 15;** ♿

This impressive Imax cinema, named after the famous Danish astronomer, shows fast-paced nature and adventure films on a 1000 sq m screen. It has a domed space theatre that offers a show of the night sky using state-of-the-art equipment.

⭐ RADIOHUSETS KONCERTSAL *Live Music*
☎ 35 20 62 62; www.dr.dk/rso/en/index **Julius Thomsensgade 1, Frederiksberg;** Ⓜ **Forum** 🚌 **2A;** ♿

Danmark Radio's 1000-seater concert house is home to Denmark's National Symphony Orchestra and national choir. Concerts usually begin at 8pm.

⭐ VEGA *Club/Live Music*
☎ 33 25 70 11; www.vega.dk; **Enghavevej 40, Vesterbro;** 🚌 **10 & 3A;** ♿

Vega is the Daddy of all Copenhagen nightlife venues yet, despite its venerable status, it remains both a cutting-edge venue for the most in-demand DJs in Europe, as well as the preferred destination of such global stars as Prince, Jamie Cullum and Arctic Monkeys. Store Vega hosts the major live acts. Lilla Vega is a great place to catch the up-and-comers of the music world and becomes the Vega Nightclub and Lounge at weekends. The Ideal Bar lets you lounge in style with a cocktail in hand and easy listening grooves as a soundtrack.

Turning Torso (p140), Malmö

>MALMÖ

If you like Copenhagen, chances are Malmö, the third-largest city in Sweden, will tickle your fancy too. This is a beautiful, lively university city, with a historic centre surrounded by a moat, two grand squares – Stortorget and Gustav Adolfs Torg – and one smaller, cosier cobbled square, Lilla Torg (the mainstream nightlife hotspot with an ice rink in winter). There are wonderful landscaped parks, an excellent art museum, a 15th-century castle filled with yet more museums and a magnificent sandy beach with a traditional cold-bathhouse. In the last five years the city's western harbour has undergone an astonishing transformation into one of the most progressive housing projects in Northern Europe, with the landmark Turning Tower by Spanish architect Santiago Calatrava at its heart.

Up until the mid-17th century this part of Sweden was actually Danish territory, so you can think of it as the Danish capital's baby brother (just don't tell the Swedes), but with an even more laidback vibe, and surprisingly buzzing nightlife thanks to a large student population. This is an even smaller city so virtually all of the main sights are within easy walking distance. But, a caveat: Malmö is a summer city to a greater extent than Copenhagen; its 270,000 inhabitants hibernate somewhat in the darker months of the year. If you are here for summer, aim for the third week in August, when over 1.6 million people visit the city for the Malmö festival to experience music, theatre and the world's largest crayfish party.

MALMÖ

◉ SEE
Malmö Konsthall............1 C4
Malmöhus Slott............2 A2

▢ SHOP
Form/Design Center......3 C2
Olson & Gerthel............4 B2
Toffelmakaren............5 C2

❙❙ EAT
Atmosfär 6 B4
Pâtisserie S:t Gertrud....7 D2
Saluhallen 8 B2
Victors 9 C2
Årstiderna i Kockska
Huset 10 C2

▼ DRINK
Centiliter och Gram......11 C2
Tempo Bar & Kök..........12 D5
Volym 13 D5

★ PLAY
Kulturbolaget................14 D5
Rundan Canal Tour......15 C2

SEE

MALMÖ KONSTHALL

☎ 040 34 12 93; www.konsthall.malmo
.se; St Johannesgatan 7; admission free;
🕑 11am-5pm Mon-Tue & Thu-Sun, to
9pm Wed; 🚌 8, 2, 5

This is one of Europe's largest art
spaces dedicated to contemporary
art, with permanent and temporary exhibitions.

MALMÖHUS SLOTT

☎ 040 34 44 38; www.malmo.se/
museer; Malmöhusvägen; adult/
consession/child 40/10Skr/free; noon-
4pm Sep-May, 10am-4pm Jun-Aug; 🚌 3

Malmö's 15th-century castle is
home to a small Naturmuseet
(Natural History Museum), Malmö
Konstmuseum (Art Museum) and
the Stadsmuseet (City Museum).
Behind is the lovely, landscaped

Kungsparken (the King's park),
with its waterways, gardens and
picnic areas.

RIBERSBORGS
KALLBADHUS

☎ 040 26 03 66; www.ribban.com;
Ribersborg Stranden; adult/child 7-17yrs
55/30Skr; 🕑 noon-7pm Mon-Fri, 9am-
4pm Sat & Sun; 🚌 3

This rickety wooden pier, dating
from 1898, offers an opportunity
to enjoy the invigorating, uniquely
Scandinavian experience of a
wood-fired sauna (with separate
male and female sections), followed by a bracing dip in the sea.

TURNING TORSO

Västra Varvsgatan, Western Harbour;
🚌 2

This controversial, 190m-high residential and conference tower was

Discover the history of Malmö within the museums of Malmöhus Slott

TELEPHONE CODES AND CURRENCY
The international dialling code for Sweden is 46, while Malmö's local code is (0) 40. Generally one Danish krone equals 1.24 Swedish kroner (Skr).

completed in November 2005 and stands in the heart of the rapidly expanding 'docklands' of Malmö's western harbour. Based on a work of sculpture by the architect himself, Spaniard Santiago Calatrava, the tower's 54 storeys twist 90 degrees as they climb upwards, creating an extraordinary effect – particularly if you stand at its base. The tower is not open to the general public but there is a gallery and small shopping centre next door.

🛍 SHOP

Malmö's main shopping area is the pedestrian Södergatan that begins at Stortorget and runs through the city centre to Gustav Adolfs Torg. From here the shops continue along Södra Förstadsgatan to Triangeln. It is all a bit provincial compared to Copenhagen, but there are some other good areas to investigate: the small but cute old town, Gamla Väster, to the west of Lilla Torg; Adelgatan and Östergatan; and the area further south, Möllevångstorget (known locally as Möllan, or 'the windmill'), with its numerous Asian grocery stores. Shopping hours are, generally, 10am to 6pm or 7pm from Monday to Friday, 10am to 3pm on Saturday and – Copenhageners take note – some shops also open noon to 4pm on Sunday.

🏛 FORM/DESIGN CENTER
Design/Homewares
☎ 040 664 51 50; www.formdesign center.com; 🕑 11am-5pm Tue- Fri, to 6pm Thu, to 4pm Sat & Sun
The exhibition space on the first floor of this historic warehouse just off Lilla Torg is dedicated to mainly Swedish design and architecture. There is a café and shop selling a range of cleverly designed clothing, textiles and homewares on the second floor.

🏛 OLSSON & GERTHEL
Homewares
☎ 040 611 7000; www.olssongerthel .se; Engelbrektsgatan 9; 🕑 11am-6pm Mon-Fri, to 4pm Sat
One of the best interior design and homeware shops in the city is just a couple of seconds away from Lilla Torg and stocks delectable European brands, including the adorable Italian Robex plasticware and Stelton gifts, plus lighting, silverware, Tivoli Audio and locally made ceramics. Just across the road is another design shop,

Formargruppen (same opening hours), selling glassware, ceramics and arts and crafts.

🔲 TOFFELMAKAREN *Footwear*
☎ 040 26 94 77; www.toffelmakaren .se; Lilla Torg 9; ⏲ 10am-6pm Mon-Fri, to 3pm Sat

This little store sells traditional and modern handmade clogs fashioned from alder tree and fine leather. It could hold the answer to all your gift needs, assuming you know the shoe size of your giftees.

🍴 EAT

Lilla Torg is the mainstream hub for bars and restaurants with Indian, Italian, Japanese, French and Swedish cuisines all represented on this pretty, cobbled square. The atmosphere in Lilla Torg on a Friday or Saturday night is flirty, friendly, a bit boisterous and loads of fun. But younger, hipper locals tend to shun Lilla Torg in favour of the area around Möllevångstorget, which has cooler DJ bars with cheaper drinks and food.

🍴 ATMOSFÄR
Modern Global €€€
☎ 040 125 077; www.atmosfar.se; Fersens väg 4; ⏲ 6pm-midnight Tue-Sun; 🚌 8, 2, 5

A menu featuring dishes such as blackened scallops with spaghetti and truffle juice suggests that

chef Henrik Regnér is striving for a different dining experience from rival Årstiderna. This is a modern, minimalist place with vast glass-plate windows and '80s black-and-white décor. The menu roams freely from Europe to Asia for its influences and the wines focus is on the Italian region of Tuscany.

🍴 PÂTISSERIE S:T GERTRUD
Patisserie €
☎ 040 630 80 80; www.sanktgertrud.se; Östergatan 7; ⏲ 7.30am-6pm Tue-Fri, 10am-4pm Sat

The city's finest cake shop sells exquisite French patisserie and is housed in a pre-Reformation cloister. There is a traditional Swedish restaurant serving a bargain fixed lunch menu and a pub, Tant Gertrud, in the same complex.

🍴 SALUHALLEN *Global* €
Lilla Torg; 10am-6pm Mon-Fri, to 4pm Sat

Situated on one of Lilla Torg's corners is this indoor lunchtime food hall with various kiosks and cafés. It is a great bet for budget food such as sushi, kebabs, seafood and Italian – just the kind of thing Copenhagen could do with, actually.

🍴 VICTORS *Swedish* €€
☎ 040 12 76 70; Lilla Torg 1; 11.30am-10.30pm Mon-Sat

This Lilla Torg landmark serves well-priced Swedish staples and transforms into a DJ bar by night. Victors has an authentic Swedish style, with stark wood panelling and simple, sturdy, minimalist furniture.

🍽 ÅRSTIDERNA I KOCKSKA HUSET
Classic Franco-Swedish   €€€€

☎ 040 230 910; www.arstiderna.se; Frans Suellsgatan 3; ⏲ 11.30am-midnight Mon-Fri, 5pm-midnight Sat
This enchanting 16th-century red-brick cellar restaurant with its vaulted ceilings and cosy corners has been considered the ultimate Malmö gourmet destination for years. And it lives up to its billing, serving seriously impeccable French-inspired food, such as fillet of veal with sweetbreads in a port wine sauce flavoured with duck's liver. Exemplary service and luscious – mostly French and Italian – wines make this every bit as good as Copenhagen's finest.

🍸 DRINK

Sweden's Draconian licensing laws mean that, aside from the government-run alcohol shops, you can only buy alcohol in restaurants, bars and hotels. The main nightlife areas are Lilla Torg, the streets around Möllevångstorget and up-coming bar haven Davidhallstorg.

🍸 CENTILITER OCH GRAM
Restaurant/Bar

☎ 040 121 812; www.centiliterochgram .se, Stortorget 17; 5pm-3am Wed-Sat
This large restaurant-bar is literally around the corner from Lilla Torg but has slightly loftier aspirations, with a doorman and a snazzier crowd. The food is contemporary European – Serrano-wrapped steak with truffle sauce, for instance – but this is more a place to drink and flirt than to eat. There is a DJ and live music most nights.

🍸 TEMPO BAR & KÖK *Bar*
☎ 040 126 021; Södra Skolegatan 30; ⏲ 4pm-1am Wed-Sun, 6pm-midnight Mon-Tue; 🚌 8, 2, 5
This DJ bar-restaurant has been pretty much the place to come of an evening for younger, ultratrendy locals (local band The Cardigans are said to be regulars behind the turntables). Close to Möllevångstorget, it is popular with students and the indie crowd.

🍸 TORSO TWISTED
Modern Scandinavian

☎ 040 126 850; www.torsotwisted.com; Västra Varvsgatan 44; ⏲ 11.30-1am Mon-Sat; 🚌 2
In the shadow of the astonishing Turning Torso tower is this equally eye-popping restaurant-bar-bistro-lounge. In this playful, stunningly designed space you

MALMÖ TRAVEL
> Distance from Copenhagen – 30km
> Direction – West
> Travel time – 35 minutes

The best way to travel to Malmö is by train. Trains leave every 20 minutes from Copenhagen Central Station to Malmö station, via Copenhagen Airport, from 5am to midnight and hourly through the night (www.dsb.dk). You can also drive, but the Øresund bridge toll for cars is quite steep (245kr each way). To reach the bridge head south out of the city, through Christianshavn and Amager, following signs along Amagerstrandvej to Copenhagen Airport. Just before the airport, signs will send you west towards the water and Malmö.

can take your pick from reasonably priced pizzas and fusion dishes in the bistro, sample wacky cocktails at the central bar area, or indulge at the bravely inventive restaurant, sampling dishes such as lobster with Jerusalem artichoke and alger, or cloudberry with vanilla, toffee and pine. The clientele walks a perilous tightrope between dressy, painfully hip and all-out pretentious, which only adds to the sense of occasion as far as we are concerned.

⭐ **VOLYM** *DJ Bar*
☎ 040 124 520; Kristianstadsgatan 7; ⌚ 4pm-1am Mon-Sat; 🚌 4, 7
One of the hottest new arrivals on the city's nightlife scene is this Spartan, youthful DJ bar close to Möllevångstorget. Like nearby Tempo Bar, it lures a fashion-conscious, young crowd with DJs, cosy candlelight, good vegetarian food and friendly New World wines.

⭐ **PLAY**
⭐ **KULTURBOLAGET** *Club*
☎ 040 302 011; www.kulturbolaget .se; Bergsgatan 18; opening hours & prices vary
The mainstay of the city's music-based nightlife scene is this 750-capacity live-music/club venue that hosts big international acts – Morrissey, Emmy-lou Harris – and heavily popular club nights on Fridays and Saturdays.

⭐ **RUNDAN CANAL TOURS** *Tours*
☎ 040 611 74 88; www.rundan.se; adult/child 75/40Skr; ⌚ every hour on the hour 11am-4pm Apr 29-Jun 22, to 7pm Jun 24-Aug 27, to 3pm Aug 28-Sep 17, noon-2pm Sep 18-Oct 1, additional 75min 9pm tour Jul 18-Aug 17
These tour boats depart on a 50-minute guided tour of the canal that circles the centre of Malmö from just opposite the Central Station and includes commentary.

WORTH THE TRIP

Within cannon range of Sweden on the Danish side of the Øresund, further north from Malmö, lies Denmark's most imposing castle, **Kronborg Slot** (☎ 49 21 30 78; www.kronborg slot .dk; adult/15-18 yrs/6-14yrs 85/60/15kr; ⏰ 11am-3pm, until 4pm at Easter and 5pm May-Sep; 🚆 Helsingør, then 10-min walk). Known to the world as Elsinore Castle and home to Shakespeare's *Hamlet*, Kronborg was built here at the entrance to the Øresund and Baltic as a grandiose tollhouse, to extract money from ships passing between the coasts of Denmark and Sweden, and also as a defensive post against fleets sailing on Copenhagen. The so-called 'Sound dues' were introduced in the 1420s by King Erik of Pomerania. He built a small fortress, Krogen, here to operate the toll. Frederik II rebuilt and enlarged the castle in a Renaissance style between 1574 and 1585 and Christian IV rebuilt it again after a fire in 1629. In 1658 the Swedes occupied the castle and took virtually everything of value from it. It was converted into barracks in 1785 and fulfilled this role until 1922, when it was opened to the public.

Today you can see the stunning 62m ballroom and other royal rooms, as well as visit the casemates and Denmark's national Maritime Museum. A stroll on the ramparts comes free of charge and, on a blue-skied spring morning, is wonderfully bracing. During the summer, Kronborg pays its respects to its most famous – largely fictional – resident, William Shakespeare's troubled teen, Hamlet. Shakespeare wrote his longest piece in 1602; scholars believe it was based on the eyewitness reports of other English actors who had visited it (there is no evidence that Shakespeare ever came here, although some of his descriptions of the castle are strikingly evocative), although two characters, Rosencrantz and Guildenstern, took their names from real Danish noblemen who had visited the English court in 1590. Every summer the castle hosts an outdoor production of the play. In the past Laurence Olivier, Richard Burton, Kenneth Branagh and Simon Russel Beale have all 'played the Dane' here.

Driving from Copenhagen, the quickest way to Helsingør is to head north on the E47/E55. But far nicer is to take the coast road, Strandvejen (route 152), which winds through the posh villas and small beaches along the exclusive Øresund coast north of the city. DSB trains to and from Copenhagen run roughly three times hourly from early morning to around midnight (66.5kr, 55 minutes).

>SNAPSHOTS

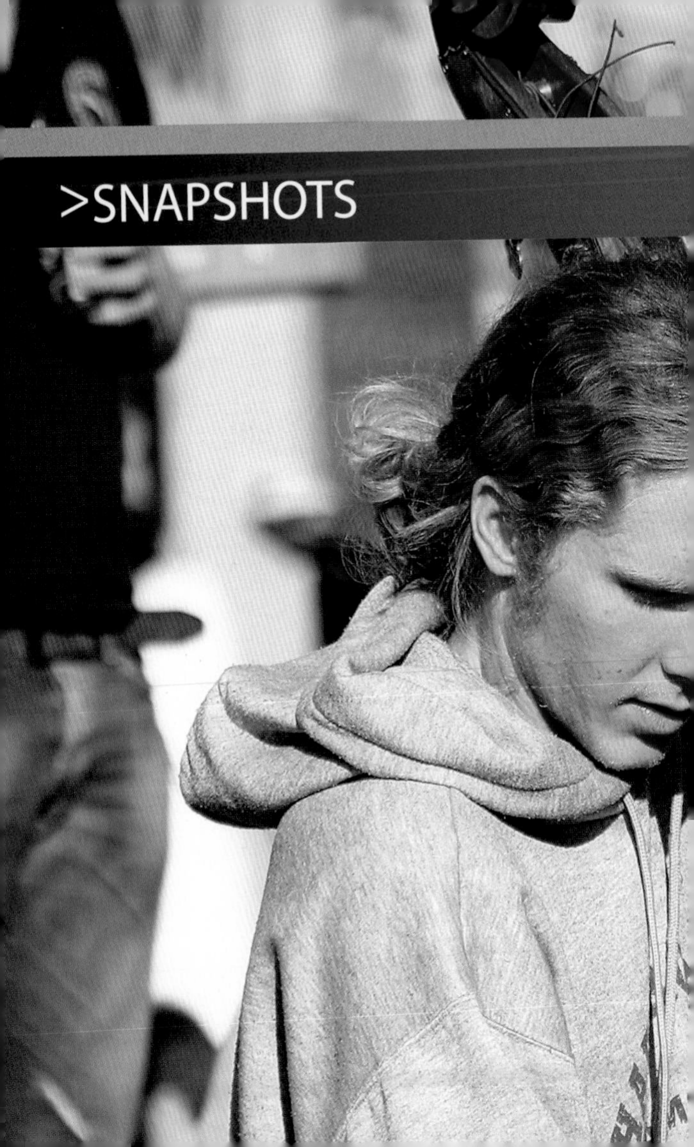

For such a small city Copenhagen has a terrific range of things to offer visitors – from a burgeoning food scene and superb accomodation options, to freewheeling travel by bike and one of the best jazz festivals in the world.

Jazz musician in Nyhavn

ACCOMMODATION

Copenhagen is enjoying a hotel boom. Room numbers have risen by 40% over the last half-decade to a total of over 13,000 today. The main growth has been in the midpriced places (1200kr to 2000kr), but the bargain end (550kr to 1000kr) has also seen considerable growth. This is not the dauntingly expensive city to stay in that it used to be.

The budget hotel area is centred on the western side of the Central Station, around Vesterbrogade and the fruitier parts of Istedgade. Slightly pricier places are to be found on and close to Rådhuspladsen while most of the posher, four- and five-star places are on the eastern side of the city centre, around Kongens Nytorv, Bredgade and the harbour.

Styles range from the experimental design of Hotel Fox, where each room is designed by a different artist (to often freaky effect), to the chintzy luxury of the celebs' favourite, the five-star Hotel d'Angleterre, and the cool, contemporary Scandinavian design of the glamorous Sankt Petri. Towering over them all is the Radisson SAS Royal, designed down to its doorknobs by Denmark's master builder, Arne Jacobsen.

The Cab-Inn chain (www.cabinn.dk) has revolutionised budget accommodation in the city in recent years and has three hotels (although, only the Cab-Inn City can truly be termed 'central'), with rooms from 525kr per person. The Danhostel organisation (www.danhostel.dk) has also shaken things up with its similarly priced, huge 'designer' hostel, Danhostel Copenhagen City, overlooking the harbour on HC Andersens Blvd. Finally, the Guldsmeden chain now has three excellent, budget-to-midrange hotels, all in Vesterbro and decorated in their French colonial style.

haystack.lonelyplanet.com

Need a place to stay? Find and book it at lonelyplanet .com. All properties featured have been personally visited, thoroughly reviewed and happily recommended by a Lonely Planet author. From hostels to high-end hotels, we've hunted out the places that will bring you unique and special experiences. Read independent reviews by authors and other travellers, and get practical information including amenities, maps and photos. Then reserve your room simply and securely via Haystack – our online booking service. It's all at lonelyplanet .com/accommodation.

The Square
COPENHAGEN

BEST
> Hotel d'Angleterre (www.remmen.dk)
> Hotel Sankt Petri (www.hotelsktpetri .dk)
> Radisson SAS Royal (www.radisson .com)
> Hotel Fox (www.hotelfox.dk)
> The Square (www.thesquare copenhagen.com)
> Hotel Front (www.front.dk)

BEST FOR THE AIRPORT
> Hilton Copenhagen Airport (www .hilton.com)

BEST BUDGET
> Cab Inn City (www.cabinn.dk)
> Danhostel Copenhagen City (www .danhostel.dk)

BEST VALUE WITH CHARACTER
> Hotel Guldsmeden chain (www .hotelguldsmeden.dk)

Opposite The exterior of the luxurious Hotel d'Angleterre **Above** View from a stylish room at The Square

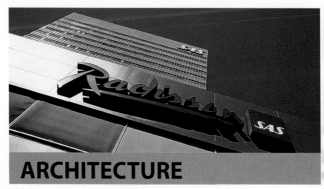

ARCHITECTURE

Copenhagen's architectural story begins at Slotsholmen and Bishop Absalon's 12th-century fortress. You can still see its ruins under Christiansborg Slot (p100).

In the early 17th century Christian IV's extraordinary building programme saw the construction of the elaborately embellished Børsen (the Stock Exchange; p100), Rundetårn (p11) and Rosenborg Slot (p15) – although at a great cost.

The ornate baroque style was a popular design for public building in the later 17th century and two splendid buildings representative of the style are Vor Frelsers Kirke (p44) in Christianshavn, and Charlottenborg (p52) at Kongens Nytorv, a former palace that now houses an art gallery.

Pre-eminent among the city's rococo structures are Amalienborg Slot's (p52) four nearly identical mansions, which were designed by architect Nicolai Eigtved at the end of the 18th century. The buildings are the residence of the royal family, but one of them is accessible to the public as a museum.

The city's leading architect of the late 19th century was Vilhelm Dahlerup, who borrowed from a broad spectrum of European Renaissance influences. His most remarkable works include Ny Carlsberg Glyptotek (p90) and the ornate Det Kongelige Teater (p62).

Some of the grander neoclassical buildings of the period are Vor Frue Kirke (p111) in the Latin Quarter and the city courthouse Domhuset (p105) on Nytorv.

Arne Jacobsen (1902–71) was a Copenhagen native and spent most of his life in his beloved city. His best-known architectural effort is the Radisson SAS Royal Hotel (p88), but he also designed the Dansk National Bank Building at Holmens Canal and a petrol station on Kystvejen in Charlottenlund, which still pumps petrol today.

The leading architect from the present day is Henning Larsen. His work includes the five-storey Dansk Design Center (p90) and the impressionists wing of the Ny Carlsberg Glyptotek. In January 2005 Copenhagen's new Opera House (p49) opened. Also by Larsen, this dazzling building features a 32m-long cantilever and six theatres.

Equally dramatic is the Royal Library extension (p101), dubbed the 'Black Diamond' (Den Sorte Diamant), which has a striking façade of black granite and smoked glass and a brilliant use of internal space. It was designed by Schmidt, Hammer and Lassen.

If you'd like to get more information about local architecture, visit the Dansk Arkitektur Center at Gammel Dok (p43).

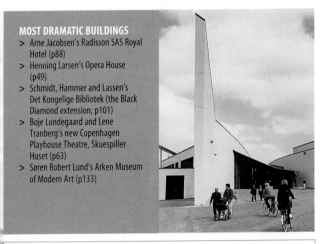

MOST DRAMATIC BUILDINGS
> Arne Jacobsen's Radisson SAS Royal Hotel (p88)
> Henning Larsen's Opera House (p49)
> Schmidt, Hammer and Lassen's Det Kongelige Bibliotek (the Black Diamond extension; p101)
> Boje Lundegaard and Lene Tranberg's new Copenhagen Playhouse Theatre, Skuespiller Huset (p63)
> Søren Robert Lund's Arken Museum of Modern Art (p133)

Opposite The attention-seeking Radisson SAS Royal **Above** The oblique angles of the Arken Museum of Modern Art

CYCLING

Copenhagen is one of the best cities in Europe for getting around by bicycle. There are separate cycle lanes along all of the main roads in Copenhagen and cycle racks everywhere you go too. No matter what the income level, age, gender, class or even weather, everyone in this city cycles. Three out of four Danes own bicycles and half use them on a regular basis.

Visitors needn't feel left out. From May to December, 1300 free City Bikes are available at 125 different locations within the city centre. To deter theft and minimise maintenance, the bicycles have a distinctive design that includes solid spokeless wheels with puncture-resistant tyres. You deposit a 20kr coin in the stand to release the bike. When you're done using the bicycle, you can return it to any stand and get your 20kr back.

Bikes can be taken on S-trains (buy a 10kr ticket from the red machine), except during weekday rush hours. You can load your bicycle in any carriage with a cycle symbol and you must stay with the bike at all times.

There are some rules worth knowing when cycling in Denmark. Cyclists give way to passengers crossing cycle lanes when embarking or disembarking at bus stops but pretty much everyone else is supposed to give way to cyclists. Cars turning right must wait for cyclists to pass them on the inside (though they obviously can't be relied upon to do this), but cyclists are not allowed to make left turns at traffic lights and larger junctions – they are supposed to dismount and cross with pedestrians before remounting and continuing.

Cycling maps, including a 1:50,000-scale map of the greater Copenhagen area, are produced by the Dansk Cyklist Forbund (Danish Cycling Federation; www.dcf.dk) and can be purchased at bookshops. For information on bicycle hire, see p171.

KIDS

If the very thought of a city break with young children has you reaching for the Valium, Copenhagen has the solution. Everywhere you go the city appears to have been geared for the little angels. Virtually all the restaurants have highchairs and many have children's menus. All the main museums offer buggies to visitors, the transport system can accommodate the largest of prams (indeed, you will notice that the Danes love those big, old Victorian-style contraptions) and there are superb play areas in all the parks. Many museums have children's sections, the theatres and music venues often have children's productions and concerts and we haven't even started on the sights and attractions created specifically for children, like the remarkable Experimentarium (p66).

The long list of kid-friendly options would surely be headed by Tivoli (p92), which has to be one of the most charming fun parks in the world. It has something for children of all ages, from pulse-quickening roller coasters and shooting galleries to sedate carousels and teacup rides. A visit to Tivoli can be an expensive affair, but there are plenty of free shows, including the famous historic Comedia dell'arte theatre, the fireworks (if they can stay up till close to midnight) and the amazing night-time lighting displays. It's also worth checking out the Buster children's film festival (www.busterfilm.dk) that overtakes city cinemas in mid-September.

BEST FOR KIDS
> Tivoli (p92)
> Zoologisk Have (p131)
> Rundetårn (p110)
> Kongens Have (p81)
> Bakken (p69)

BEST FOR A RAINY DAY
> DGI-Byen (p136)
> Imax Tycho Brahe Planetarium (p136)
> Zoologisk Museum (p67)
> Experimentarium (p66)
> Nationalmuseet (p90)

HYGGE

We realise it is a little unusual for a guidebook to dedicate a full page to a feeling, but in the case of the Danish *hygge* we heartily recommend that you grab a bit of the action. So what is *hygge*? Usually it is translated as 'cosy' but *hygge* means much more than that. *Hygge* refers to a sense of friendly, warm companionship of a kind fostered when Danes gather together in groups of two or more, although you can actually *hygge* yourself if there is no one else around. The participants don't even have to be friends (indeed, you might only just have met), but if the conversation flows – avoiding potentially divisive topics like politics and the best method to pickle herring – the bonhomie blossoms, toasts are raised before an open fire (or at the very least, some candles), you are probably coming close. Happily, Copenhagen's restaurants, cafés and bars do their utmost to foster a *hyggelige* atmosphere, with open fires, candles lit no matter what time of day or year and, of course, a nonstop supply of alcohol (which is sold in virtually all cafés). Listed below are some of the best places to experience that *hygge* vibe.

BEST HYGGE CAFÉS
> Bastionen og Løven (p46)
> Bang og Jensen (p134)
> La Glace (p122)
> Tea Time (p74; pictured right)
> Café Wilder (p46)

BEST HYGGE BARS
> Bibendum (p87)
> Bankeråt (p86)
> Fisken (p62)
> Café Bopa (p72)
> Sofie Kælderen (p48)

SHOPPING

What Copenhagen's shopping portfolio lacks in size it more than makes up for with quality and individuality. If you are bored with mass-produced, chain store designs, the side streets and offbeat shopping areas of the city have the answer. Of course, Copenhagen has all the big retail names and some homegrown heavyweights – Illums Bolighus (p117), Bodum (p113) and Bang & Olufsen (p55) among them – which are mostly centred on the main pedestrian shopping street, Strøget. However, the city's real strength lies in its young designers, working alone or in small collectives and selling their clothes, interior design items, ceramics and glassware from their own shops. They're predominantly in Vesterbro (p128) and Nørrebro (p64), but also in the areas north and south of Strøget between Kongens Nytorv and Købmagergade, and on Strædet (p111).

The first thing you need to know about shopping in Copenhagen is that, as fantastic as its shops are, shopping is very much a privilege, not a right, in Denmark. There are strict laws governing how many hours and days a week shops can open and, as difficult as it might be to deal with for those used to the 24/7 spending opportunities in London or New York, most shops close early on Saturdays and few, aside from local grocers, ever open on a Sunday. That said, many shops do stay open late (until 7pm or 8pm) on Fridays. And for Sunday shopping, there is always Malmö (p138).

Visitors from countries outside the EU who buy goods in Denmark can get a refund of the 25% VAT, less a handling fee, if they spend at least 300kr at any retail outlet that participates in the 'Tax Free Shopping Global Refund' plan. This includes most shops catering for tourists. The 300kr can be spent on a single item or several items as long as they are purchased from the same shop. Visit www.globalrefund.com for more information.

MUSIC

Copenhagen has a small, lively music scene with some impressive venues, all offering a wide range of classical, jazz, opera, pop and rock music. You can catch a live-music performance of some sort or other most nights of the week, whether it be a late-night jazz jam at La Fontaine (p127), a lavish, cutting edge Cosi Fan Tutti at the Opera House (p49) or a major chart star at Vega (p136). Major international acts such as Madonna and Bob Dylan have recently taken to playing in Jutland over the capital, but venues such as Forum (p136) and the national stadium Parken (p77) still attract big stars.

In terms of homegrown acts, Denmark's biggest-selling piece of music ever is 'Barbie Girl' by the blessedly defunct Aqua, which sold 28 million copies in the late 1990s. It was the first major international hit by a Danish artist since Whigfield's 'Saturday Night', which wasn't exactly a track record to be proud of, but a small trickle of better quality Danish acts have followed, including Kashmir (often compared to Radiohead), Tim Christensen (a talented folk-rock singer/songwriter), The Raveonettes (Denmark's answer to The White Stripes) and prog-rock outfit Mew, all of whom have enjoyed significant overseas sales in recent years. The Danish DJ and remix scene is centred on Copenhagen and is buoyant with acts like SoulShock, Cutfather and Junior Senior achieving some success abroad.

The **Roskilde Festival** (www.roskildefestival.dk; 2008 3-6 Jul; 2009 2-5 Jul; ticket in 2007 1475kr; 🚆 Roskilde, festival bus) takes place every summer and offers a stunning range of live music. 2007's festival saw bands as diverse as Wilco, Slayer and Muse, not to mention a large range of Scandinavian bands, take the stage; see also p20.

TOP FIVE COPENHAGEN SOUNDTRACKS

> 'Wonderful Copenhagen' (Danny Kaye) Don't pretend you haven't been singing this to yourself since you got here…
> 'Barbie Girl' (Aqua) As soothing as a foghorn and as subtle as a brick, it remains one of Denmark's biggest global hits.
> 'Love In A Trashcan' (The Raveonettes) The lead single from the duo's 2005 album *Pretty In Black*.
> 'Played-A-Live (The Bongo Song)' (Safri Duo). Idiotic drum anthem from the classically trained Danish percussionists, who ought to know better.
> 'Fly On the Wings of Love' (Olsen Brothers) 2000 Eurovision winner. Denmark's proudest moment since… well, possibly ever.

JAZZ

Jazz arrived in Copenhagen in the mid-1920s and it didn't take long for a strong local scene to grow up around the clubs in the city. Major international jazz stars such as Louis Armstrong and Django Reinhardt were drawn to the Danish capital by its enthusiastic, knowledgeable audiences; Stan Getz, Dexter Gordon and Ben Webster even lived in the city during the peak of their careers. After WWII Copenhagen came to be considered the jazz capital of Scandinavia and its legendary Montmartre Club was one of the most famous jazz venues in Europe. The Montmartre doesn't exist any more but clubs such as the intimate La Fontaine (p127), now the oldest and most 'hard core' jazz club in the city, as well as smaller venues like Huset (p127), ensure that legacy remains vibrant.

Many of the city's other music venues such as Tivoli's Koncertsal (p97) and even the Opera House (p49) turn their hand to jazz from time to time – particularly during July's Copenhagen Jazz Festival (p21), but the undisputed titan of the city's jazz scene today is the Copenhagen Jazzhouse (p126), located just north of central Strøget. This two-storey venue hosts live performances encompassing a wide range of jazz genres and featuring international and domestic stars, often followed by club nights on the intimate basement dance floor. Together with Vega (p136) it is one of the most consistent live-music venues in the city.

Copenhagen is still home to a large group of both homegrown and international jazz musicians. The living legend of the Copenhagen jazz scene is 91-year-old Svend Asmussen, who has played with the likes of Benny Goodman, Fats Waller and Django Reinhardt in his time. He still plays in Copenhagen occasionally, as does veteran trumpeter Palle Mikkelberg. If you are interested in learning more about the jazz scene in Copenhagen and taking in a few clubs, you might enjoy a Copenhagen Jazz Tour (p178).

BEST JAZZ FESTIVAL VENUES
> Copenhagen Jazzhouse (www.copenhagenjazzhouse.dk)
> La Fontaine (www.lafontaine.dk)
> Mojo (www.mojo.dk)
> Huset (www.huset.dk)
> Vega (www.vega.dk; pictured right)

SEASONAL COPENHAGEN

With weather as extreme as Copenhagen's can be, the seasons can have a significant impact on a visit. That is not to say you shouldn't come here in the winter; there are pluses as well as minuses at this time of year, particularly at Christmas time. Copenhagen lays on a fantastic Christmas: the decorations come out on Strøget's shopping strips, Tivoli (p92) opens with its special brand of seasonal schmaltz and the cafés do a roaring trade in mulled red wine and roaring fires. Heavy snow rarely hinders the locals from getting on with things, so you needn't worry about finding yourself hotel-bound, just do make sure you have enough clothing with you. We don't want to sound like your mother here, but you can get some excellent winter sports clothing in the outdoors shops on Frederiksborggade and there is nothing like an Icelandic woollen to keep the chill out. Also, from the end of November to February there is a free open-air ice skating rink on Kongens Nytorv, as well as similar rinks at Frederiksberg Runddel and Blågårds Plads in Nørrebro.

That said, most people seem to agree that the best time to visit Copenhagen is between May and August. As soon as the sun starts to radiate a little warmth, an extraordinary change comes over the city. The locals cast off their clothes, take to the outdoor café tables en masse and, at the weekend, really let their hair down with numerous festivals (p20), outdoor music and, it has to be said, liver-shrivelling amounts of alcohol. They even go swimming in the harbour (see p48). Be warned: Copenhagen does go a little dead in late July, when the entire city seems to leave for their summer houses and some of the better restaurants close.

OMANTIC COPENHAGEN

t takes quite a lot to maintain a façade of romance when the tempera-
ure is touching -15°C, you're up to your knees in slushy, muddy snow,
nd wrapped up like the Michelin Man, but somehow, against the odds,
Copenhagen is a deeply romantic city, even in winter. Consider a walk
hrough a frosty Dyrehaven (p69), then back to town for a mulled wine
eside the open fire in Cap Horn (p58), and dinner at Alberto K (p94) as
ou watch the lights in Sweden gently twinkling. Come springtime and
he options multiply exponentially, not least because you can now dress
ike a human instead of a walrus. The cafés and restaurants move their
ables outside, the flowers blossom in Frederiksberg Have (p130) and the
azz Festival (p21) gives you all the excuse you need to sweep your lover
p in to your arms and spin him/her around the dance floor.

BEST ROMANTIC RESTAURANTS
> Alberto K (p94)
> Restaurant Kanalen (p48)
> The Paul (p95)
> Restaurant d'Angleterre (p59)
> Les Trois Cochons (p133)

BEST ROMANTIC WALKS
> Tivoli (p92), but only after dark
> Kongens Have (p81), but not if the
  sunbathers are out
> Frederiksberg Have (p130), but only
  if it's springtime
> Dyrehaven (p69), but only when it's
  frosty
> Langelinie to the Little Mermaid
  (p54), but only if the wind isn't
  blowing

SNAPSHOTS

TRADITIONAL FOOD

For all the hype and hullabaloo surrounding modern Scandinavian cooking, the truth is that most Danes are a conservative bunch when it comes to food. Even though Copenhageners – particularly the younger ones – are dining out more and more, their compatriots generally prefer homecooked, stout fare. Dishes heavy on pork are invariably accompanied by potatoes in one form or another, and *brun sovs*, a kind of gravy. *Frikadeller*, the traditional Danish meatball, are a mixture of ground beef and pork eaten by every Dane at least a couple of times a month. Meanwhile, pickled herring *(sild)*, remains the staple of the *kolde bord* (cold table, Denmark's answer to the Swedish Smorgasboard).

As you might have guessed, the Danish diet is not an especially healthy one. They eat large quantities of animal foods, processed foods and dairy produce. Breakfast often consists of pastries, cheese and cured meats. Traditionally, the favourite fast food is hot dogs from the *pølser vogner* (sausage wagons) that station themselves around the city, all churning out precisely the same frankfurter, buns and dressings (although, we have to admit, occasionally a *pølser* slathered with fake mustard and ketchup can really hit the spot). Interesting foodstuffs to try or take home include pickled herring, salami, smoked fish, local cheeses and akvavit, the 40%-proof herbed potato spirit, which does a good job of numbing the palate before you eat.

BEST FOR TRADITIONAL DANISH FOOD

> Ida Davidsen (p59; pictured right)
> Slotskælderen Hos Gitte Kik (p123)
> Huset med det Grønne Træ (p122)
> Peder Oxe (p122)
> Restaurant Kanalen (p48)

NEW FOOD

A few years ago Copenhagen would have been the last place on earth to recommend food-lovers to visit. Today Copenhagen has more Michelin stars than any other Scandinavian city. What has turned this culinary backwater into a burgeoning culinary destination?

The answer is: its young chefs, many of whom have trained at prestigious, progressive restaurants around Europe and the US. These chefs, including Noma's (p47) Rene Redzepi and Prémisse's (p59) Rasmus Grønbech, have taken their experience and combined it with a passion for Denmark's local raw ingredients – its excellent pork, game, seafood, wild mushrooms, berries etc – and an almost religious observance of the seasons. One measure of the new seriousness with which Danes approach the business of food is the instant success of their first food festival, Copenhagen Cooking (p28). Fresh arrivals on the Copenhagen dining scene include Tivoli's Brasserie 'N' and award-winning chef Rasmus Kofoed's Geranium, which promises to be among the very best the city has to offer. So the New Danish food revolution is in full swing and that can only be good news for tourists, particularly as the number of places with outdoor seating has almost quadrupled in the last decade. One benefit, at least, of global warming.

BEST FOR MODERN NORDIC COOKING
> Noma (p47)
> Prémisse (p59)
> Restaurant d'Angleterre (p59)

BEST DÉCOR
> Umami (p61)
> The Custom House (p61)

BEST FOREIGN
> Ebisu (p61)
> Wokshop Cantina (p62)
> Lê Lê Nhà Hàng (p133)
> Sticks 'n' Sushi (p84)

BEST BUDGET
> Rizraz (p123)
> Lê Lê Nhà Hàng (p133)
> Wokshop Cantina (p62)
> Cofoco (p132)
> Morgenstedet (p47)

BEST FOR FRENCH
> Cofoco (p132)
> Les Trois Cochons (p133)
> Restaurant d'Angleterre (p59)

BEST FOR DINING IN SOMEONE'S KITCHEN
> 1.th (p57)

GAY LIFE

Copenhagen is a popular gay getaway. Gays and lesbians are totally accepted in Danish society and there is a small but active gay scene here – predominantly, it has to be said, focused on gay men. The Landsforeningen for Bøsser and Lesbiske (Union of Gays and Lesbians; www.ldl.dk) was founded back in 1948 to promote gay rights, with great success – Denmark was the first country to legalise gay marriage, and adoption by gay couples is also allowed.

The main gay and lesbian festival is Copenhagen Pride (www.copenhagen-pride.dk), a Mardi Gras–style bash held on a Saturday in early August. The Copenhagen Gay & Lesbian Film Festival (www.cglff.dk) is held each year in October. The most popular gay cruising area in the city is HC Ørsteds Park. In 2009 the city will host the second World Outgames – the gay Olympics (www.copenhagen2009.org). For more information on the scene in Copenhagen visit www.copenhagen-gay-life.dk and www.gayguide.dk.

BEST GAY VENUES
> Pan Disco (p127)
> Boiz (p127)
> Can Can (Mikkel Bryggersgade)
> CentralHjørnet (www.centralhjornet.dk)
> Jailhouse (p125)

Off to visit the Queen at Amalienborg Slot on Dronning Margrethe II's Birthday

BACKGROUND

HISTORY

FOUNDING OF COPENHAGEN

In 1167 Bishop Absalom constructed a fortress on Slotsholmen to protect against pirates from the Baltic. In the years that followed, the harbourside village expanded and took on the name Københavnshavn (Merchant's Port). The port did much of its trade in salted herring, which was in high demand, in part due to the religious restrictions against eating meat during Catholic holy days, such as Lent.

In 1376 construction began on a new Slotsholmen fortification. King Erik of Pomerania took up residence at the castle in 1416, marking the beginning of Copenhagen's role as the capital of Denmark.

A pivotal power struggle involving the monarchy and the Catholic church was played out during the Danish Reformation. Frederik I ascended the throne in 1523 and invited Lutheran preachers to Denmark. Their fiery messages against the corrupt power of the Catholic church found a ready ear among the disenchanted. The country, already strained by social unrest, erupted into civil war in 1534. Eventually the Danish Lutheran church was established as the only state-sanctioned denomination.

It was during the reign of Christian IV (1588–1648) that Copenhagen was endowed with much of its splendour. Christian ascended the throne at the age of 10 and ruled for more than 50 years. Many of Copenhagen's most lavish buildings were erected during his reign. The king also extended the city significantly, developing the district of Christianshavn, which he modelled on Amsterdam. Among the many grand buildings that have survived through the centuries are Børsen (p100), Rosenborg Slot (p82) and the Rundetårn (p110).

Unfortunately, the king's foreign policies weren't nearly as brilliant. He dragged Denmark into a protracted struggle that came to be known as the Thirty Years' War. On 26 February 1658 the Treaty of Roskilde, the most lamented treaty in Denmark's history, was signed by his successor, Frederik III. The territorial losses were staggering, with Denmark's borders shrinking by one-third.

In 1728 a sweeping fire razed most of Copenhagen's medieval buildings, levelling one-third of the city, including the centre of government at Slotsholmen. A new and grander edifice, Christiansborg Slot, was built to replace it, and the city began to rebuild. Then in 1795 a second fire ravaged the city's remaining timber buildings, destroying the final remnants of Absalon's medieval town and the new Christiansborg Slot as well.

Copenhagen recovered from this fire only to be bombarded by the British navy in both 1801 and 1807 – resentment still lingers over that one.

By the 1830s Copenhagen had awakened to a cultural revolution in the arts, philosophy and literature, and adopted its first democratic constitution, enacted on 5 June 1849.

At the same time Copenhagen, which had previously been under royal administration, was granted the right to form a municipal council. Copenhagen's boundaries were extended into the districts of Østerbro, Vesterbro and Nørrebro to accommodate the city's growth and the new working class.

WWII

Denmark declared neutrality at the outbreak of WWII but in the early hours of 9 April 1940 the Germans landed troops at strategic points throughout Denmark. Despite the occupation, Copenhagen and the rest of Denmark emerged from WWII relatively unscathed.

Postwar Denmark saw the establishment of a comprehensive social-welfare system under the leadership and guidance of the Social Democrats.

During WWII and in the economic depression that had preceded it, many Copenhagen neighbourhoods had deteriorated into slums. In 1948 an ambitious urban renewal policy called the 'Finger Plan' was adopted and redeveloped much of the city, creating new housing projects interspaced with green areas of parks and recreational facilities that spread out like fingers from the city centre.

Denmark's monarchy continues to move with the times while providing a stable sense of tradition. In May 2004 Crown Prince Frederik and Mary Donaldson married, turning the entire city of Copenhagen into a giant party.

THE DANISH FLAG

The Danish flag, or *Dannebrog*, is said to be the world's oldest national flag. Legend says the first *Dannebrog* fell from the sky during a battle against the Estonians in 1219, which certainly saved on the design costs.

In 2006 Denmark experienced what Prime Minister Anders Fogh Rasmussen called the most serious crisis since WWII when the Muslim world reacted with violent protests and bans on Danish goods when the Danish right-wing newspaper, *Jyllands Posten*, published cartoons depicting the Prophet Mohammed.

VISUAL ARTS

Copenhagen is the undisputed centre of the Danish contemporary art scene. In Christianshavn and Islands Brygge in particular, you can't throw a paintbrush without hitting an artist of some kind (though probably not the kind who uses a paintbrush). Leading the pack is Olafur Eliasson, best known for his Weather Project installation in Tate Modern. Funding ensures that the artist starving in a garret is a rare thing in Denmark and there are dozens of galleries and public art spaces in the city, including Charlottenborg (p52), Overgaden (p43) and Kunstforeningen (p108).

Some refer to the present day as the new 'Golden Age' of Danish art, referring to the first half of the 19th century when artists such as Christoffer Eckersberg (1783–1853) and Christian Købke (1810–48) painted scenes of everyday life with startling clarity and power. You can see paintings from this period in Statens Museum for Kunst (p82) and Den Hirschsprungske Samling (p80). The leading sculptor of the day was Bertel Thorvaldsen (1770–1844), who spent most of his working life in Rome producing work inspired by classical antiquity. When he returned to Copenhagen he established his own museum (p103). Another important art movement that evolved in the Danish capital was Cobra (formed by artists in Copenhagen, Brussels and Amsterdam), formed in 1948 by, among others, the Danish abstract artist Asger Jørn (1914–73). There are several Cobra pieces in Statens Museum (p82) and Louisiana Museum for Modern Art (p66).

DESIGN

Never consciously fashionable, but always ahead of contemporary trends, Danish designers offer a distinctive brand of simple, pared-down beauty and functionality in industrial design. Early 20th-century design pioneers such as Georg Jensen (p117) paved the way for global design leaders such as Hans J Wegner, Arne Jacobsen and Verner Panton. Wegner's 1948 Round Chair, with its simple, smooth curving lines, is often cited as a prime example of Danish design. A decade later Arne Jacobsen produced his iconic Ant Stacker Chair, made from plywood and steel tubing. Indeed, if there is one item of furniture the Danes are famous for perfecting it is the Stacker Chair. Panton refined the genre to perhaps its ultimate incarnation in the Panton Chair, made in a variety of pop art colours from a single piece of plastic. Danish designers excelled in the field of lighting too – Poul Henningsen's designs still look futuristic today.

Danish design brought an organic sensibility to the functionalism of Bauhaus while simultaneously giving the arts and crafts movement a modernist makeover. The result has been not just great artistic acclaim, but big business. Brands like Lego, Bang and Olufsen, Bodum, Georg Jensen and Royal Copenhagen Porcelain are revered around the world. Excellent design venues include Danish Design Center (p90) and Kunstindustrimuseet (p53) in the antique stores on Bredgade and Ravnsborggade, but the best place to see Danish design is in its natural environment: in a Danish home. For the Danes, good design is not just for museums and institutions; they live with it day to day.

ENVIRONMENT

The Danes are an environmentally conscious people. They use public transport and cycle to a far greater extent than most of the rest of Europe. In 1971 Denmark was the first country to set up an Environment ministry. All but 8km of the 5,000km coastline is safe and clean to swim in, the people have been avid recyclers since the 1970s (by 2008 Denmark aims to recycle 65% of its waste) and it currently produces around 20% of its power from wind turbines.

It is these turbines – 'windmills' seems too quaint a word for these giant, futuristic wind-blade towers, a row of which can be seen from planes landing at Copenhagen just east of the harbour – that has led Denmark to become globally associated with environmentally friendly initiatives. It is the world's biggest producer of wind turbines and the Danish energy sector is hoping to produce 50% of its energy this way by 2025.

On a slightly less happy note, the ammonia from pig manure produced by the huge pig-farming industry (there are 13 million pigs in Denmark, compared to five-and-a-half million people) is problematic and the smoking habit still lingers. About 25% of Danes over 13 smoke regularly. Over 12,000 of them die each year as a result of smoking-related illnesses. In April 2007 a rather tame new law banning smoking in public buildings came into force – but even the queen, a famous heavy smoker, now refrains from lighting up while on official duties.

GOVERNMENT AND POLITICS

Denmark is a constitutional monarchy. It has a single chamber parliamentary system with 179 MPs and a befuddling array of political parties. The Danes prefer a political system based on consensus and compromise or, at least, they used to. In 2001 the Danes elected Anders Fogh Rasmussen, of the Venstre Party (Liberal – literally this translates as the 'left' party, although, confusingly, they are right-wing) to power. Not having enough seats to command a majority, Rasmussen (once called the most handsome leader in Europe, albeit by Silvio Berlusconi), has been saddled with a coalition in which Denmark's third-largest party, the rather unsavoury Folke Parti (People's Party), wields a great deal of power.

The Folke Parti is obsessed with immigration – talk to many Copenhageners and they will tell you that, essentially, the party's leadership will buy into any reactionary, fear-based policies they think will win them votes with the educationally challenged yokels of Jutland (and their youth wing is notoriously extreme). The fear of losing their support led Rasmussen to impose some of the most Draconian immigration legislation in Europe (although it doesn't seem to apply to pretty Tasmanian girls with royal links).

The Folke Parti made much capital from the greatest political crisis to strike the country in recent years: the Mohammed Cartoons affair (2006), in which a right-wing Jutland newspaper published deliberately inflammatory (and worse, not very funny) cartoons of the Prophet Mohammed. A few months later, a Copenhagen-based imam lit the touch paper by showing them to some friends in Saudi Arabia, and Danish flag-making companies enjoyed a windfall as the *Dannebrog* (Danish flag) was burned in the streets in cities throughout the Middle East. That has all calmed down now, of course, but this little fairy-tale nation was in deep shock for some months after. Denmark was judged to have lost €134 million in trade to the Middle East, although exports to the USA rose by 17% in the first quarter of 2006.

FURTHER READING

Just as Danish art enjoyed a Golden Age in the first half of the 19th century, so too did its literature. It came with the emergence of its national poet, Adam Ohlenschläger, a romantic lyric poet and playwright, and Hans Christian Andersen (p93), who turned his hand to just about every literary form from poems to travel writing, but was of course most famous

TOP FIVE COPENHAGEN READS

> *The Complete Fairy Tales* (Hans Christian Andersen) The most famous Danish book in the world. Several of the stories describe real places in the city.
> *Either/Or* (Søren Kierkegaard) The first great work of the father of existentialism.
> *Miss Smilla's Feeling for Snow* (Peter Høeg). A world-wide hit set largely in Christianshavn, later filmed with Julia Ormond and Richard Harris.
> *Silence in October* (Jens Christian Grøndahl) An engaging meditation on the dissolution of a marriage, as a man pieces together his wife's disappearance and his own inner life. Features numerous Copenhagen locations, especially around the city lakes.
> *Prince* (Ib Michael) Denmark's leading exponent of magic realism – this was his first novel translated into English.

For more information on Danish writers, visit www.literaturenet.dk.

or his fairy tales. Other poets of the time included Nicolaj Frederik Severin Grundtvig – still an important literary figure in Denmark – and Bernhard Severin Ingemann.

Another important Golden Age figure was Søren Kierkegaard (p109), whose first published work was actually a criticism of one of Andersen's novels (it was not an easy read and at the time it was claimed that only two people had read it – the author and Andersen). Around 1870 a trend towards realism emerged, focusing on contemporary issues. One of the leading figures of this new movement, Henrik Pontoppidan, won a Nobel Prize for Literature in 1917 for his epic *The Realm of the Dead*. He was joined the same year by Karl Adolph Gjellerup, and in 1944 by Johannes Vilhelm Jensen.

The most famous Danish writer of the 20th century, Karen Blixen, was also nominated for the prize. She is best known for her memoir, *Out of Africa* (made into an Oscar-winning film starring Meryl Streep and Robert Redford). One of Denmark's leading contemporary novelists is the reclusive Peter Høeg, a former ballet dancer who had a global hit with *Miss Smilla's Feeling for Snow* in 1992. This was also made into a film, directed by Bille August. Several of Høeg's works have been translated into English.

In the last decade two English writers have taken Copenhagen and its more famous residents for their theme: Rose Tremain's *Music and Silence* tells of the troubled later life of King Christian IV, while Michael Frayn's play, *Copenhagen*, imagines what went on between nuclear physicists Niels Bohr and Werner Heisenberg during WWII.

DIRECTORY
TRANSPORT
ARRIVAL & DEPARTURE
AIR

The city's international airport is **Copenhagen Kastrup** (☎ 33 21 32 31; www .cph.dk), located at the southeastern tip of the island of Amager, southeast of the city centre. You can fly to Kastrup from several UK airports including Gatwick, Heathrow, Stansted, London City, Manchester, Belfast and Edinburgh. There are three terminals at Kastrup: Terminal 1 is for domestic flights, and Terminals 2 and 3 are for international flights. Be sure to check which one you are arriving at and departing from, although they are only a three-minute walk apart.

The quickest and cheapest way to get to the western side of the city centre is to take the train that leaves from beneath Terminal 3 and whisks you into the Central Station in 12 minutes. A one-way ticket is 28.5kr. At the Central Station you can change to the local S-tog (S-train) service, which has 13 lines serving the city centre and suburbs.

Note that the metro does not pass through the Central Station, but the metro line from the eastern side of the city centre to Amager is due to be extended to Terminal 3 of the airport in October 2007.

There is a taxi rank outside Terminal 3. The ride into the city centre costs around 200kr and takes about 20 minutes.

All the major car-hire companies have offices in the airport.

Malmö airport is well outside Malmö and over an hour away by bus from central Copenhagen.

TRAIN

All train services – whether from Sweden, via the Øresund Bridge, or from Germany – stop at Central

CLIMATE CHANGE & TRAVEL

Travel – especially air travel – is a significant contributor to global climate change. At Lonely Planet, we believe that all who travel have a responsibility to limit their personal impact. As a result, we have teamed with Rough Guides and other concerned industry partners to support Climate Care, which allows people to offset the greenhouse gases they are responsible for with contributions to energy-saving projects and other climate-friendly initiatives in the developing world. Lonely Planet offsets all staff and author travel.

For more information, turn to the responsible travel pages on www.lonelyplanet .com. For details on offsetting your carbon emissions, and a carbon calculator, go to www .climatecare.org.

ROAD, SEA & RAIL

As an alternative to flying to Copenhagen you could travel here by boat or train. If you are coming from Scandinavia, for instance, you could catch the ferry from Oslo to Copenhagen (☎ 33 42 30 00; www.dfdsseaways.com), or from Helsingborg, in Sweden, to Helsingør, 40 minutes north of Copenhagen by train (HH Ferries; ☎ 49 26 01 55; www.hhferries.dk; Scandlines; ☎ 33 15 15 15; www.scandlines.dk). Ferries leave every 20 minutes during the day and hourly at night. Ferries to Swinoujscie in Poland leave from Nordhavn (the northern harbour) and take about 10 hours (Polferries; ☎ +46 40 97 61 80; www.polferries.se). From Germany it is just five hours by train from Hamburg to Copenhagen Central Station, via the boat-train from Puttgarden to Rødby (DSB; ☎ 70 13 14 15; www.dsb.dk). From Britain, you can sail with DFDS from Harwich to Esbjerg on Jutland, and then take the train direct to Copenhagen – there are sailings 3-4 times per week. The trip from London to Copenhagen, including trains, takes about 25 hours.

Eurolines Scandinavia runs a bus service to and from Stockholm and Gothenburg (☎ 70 10 00 30; www.eurolines.dk; Halmtorvet 5, Vesterbro). Buses leave from Ingerslevsgade near the Central Station. Tickets must be bought in advance either via the internet or at the Halmtorvet office.

tation. For all train enquiries contact **DSB** (☎ 70 13 14 15; www.dsb.dk).

GETTING AROUND

You are best off on foot within the heart of the city centre as much of it is pedestrianised and bus-free. That said, Copenhagen's exceptional, modern transport network, served by buses, the metro and S-train, is one of its trump cards. For information on public transport within the city (on S-train and bus) visit www.rejseplanen.dk, which includes an integrated route planner for bus, metro, train and S-train.

CITY BIKES

From April to November Copenhagen Council makes 1300 free bicycles available at 110 bike racks throughout the city centre. You leave a 20kr deposit in the slot, as with a supermarket trolley, and away you go – you get your money back when you return the bike to any bike rack.

One of the most convenient rental options is at **Københavns Cykler** (Map p129, D3; ☎ 33 33 86 13; www .rentabike.dk; Reventlowsgade 11; per day 75-200kr; ⊙ 8am-5.30pm Mon-Fri, 9am-1pm Sat, 10am-1pm Sun during summer; ⓡ Central Station), in the basement of Central Station. The bicycles are in good working order and children's seats are available for hire. A deposit of 500 to1000kr is required. The bike cost reduces per day the more days you rent.

TICKETS & TRAVEL PASSES

As you would expect, this integrated network has a ticket system based on seven geographical zones. Most of your travel will probably be within two zones. Single tickets are valid for one hour's travel (adult/child aged 12-15 1 to 2 zones 19/9.5kr; 3 zones 28.5/19kr; children under 12 travel free if accompanied by an adult). Also available are discount 10-ticket cards (adult/child 1 to 2 zones 120/66kr; 3 zones 160/80kr), which you must stamp in the yellow machines when boarding buses or on the train/metro platforms. Tickets are valid for travel on the metro, buses and S-train (even though they may look slightly different, depending on where you buy them). One ticket allows you to travel for one hour on all three types of transport.

If you buy a Copenhagen Card (p174), all travel on local public transport is inclusive.

METRO

The driverless trains of Copenhagen's **metro** (☎ 33 11 17 00; www .m.dk; ☺ 5am-midnight Sun-Wed, 24hr Thu-Sat) whoosh passengers from the western city suburb of Vanløse through the eastern side of the city centre and on to Amager. Trains run at intervals varying from every two minutes to every 15 minutes, depending on the time of day. The main stations of interest for visitors to the city will be Nørreport, Kongens Nytorv and Christianshavn. The two lines, M1 and M2, diverge at Christianshavn. By October 2007 the M1 line should be able to take you all the way from Kongens Nytorv to the airport in 13 minutes.

S-TRAIN

The local S-train runs from the suburbs through the city centre via Østerport, Nørreport, Vesterport and the Central Station. Please note that Vesterport Station is almost within sight of the Central Station. There are 13 S-train lines/routes and services run from around 5am to midnight to 1am. For information visit www.dsb.dk. The S-train does not run to Copenhagen Airport, which is a mainline station (the last before trains cross the Øresund Bridge to Sweden).

The S-train is part of the integrated ticket zone system, together with the buses and metro, so one ticket covers you on transport on any of these three forms of transport within one hour of purchase and within the zones covered by the ticket. See Tickets and Travel passes (left) for prices.

RAIL TRAVEL TO SWEDEN

Malmö is just 40 minutes by train from Copenhagen Central Station.

For information on mainline rail destinations and train travel to Sweden visit www.rejseplanen.dk or telephone DSB.

BUS

Buses run day and night in Copenhagen. The night service is more expensive and less frequent and runs from 1am to 5am. Copenhagen's yellow HT buses are part of the integrated ticket zone system together with the metro and S-train, so one ticket covers you on transport on any of these three forms of transport within one hour of purchase. See Tickets and Travel passes (opposite) for prices.

Copenhagen's buses are run by Arriva. Unfortunately, the website www.movia.dk is only in Danish. They do have a phone inquiries line (☎ 70 27 74 820), but no guarantee that the person who answers will speak English. However, you can plan bus trips in and around the capital at www rejseplanen.dk, which has an English-language option.

TAXI

Taxis can be flagged on the street and there are ranks at various points around the city centre. If the yellow Taxa sign is lit, the taxi is available for hire. The fare will start at 19kr (32kr if you have ordered it by phone) and costs

10.2kr per km 7am to 4pm, 11.2kr 4pm to 7am Monday to Friday, 13kr 11pm to 7am Friday and Saturday, 11kr Sunday and public holidays. Most taxis accept major credit cards. Four of the main companies are:

Codan Taxi (☎ 70 25 25 25)
Hovedstadens Taxi (☎ 38 77 77 77)
Taxa 4x35 (☎ 35 35 35 35)
Taxamotor (☎ 38 10 10 10)

BICYCLE RICKSHAW

During the summer, you can hail a **Quickshaw** (☎ 35 43 01 22; www.rickshaw .dk) or a **bicycle taxi** (☎ 70 26 00 55; www.cykeltaxi.com) for travel within the city centre. Fares vary.

HARBOUR BUSES

The **harbour boat-bus service** (☎ 36 13 14 15; www.movia.dk) runs from the Black Diamond (Det Kongelige Bibiliotek) to Nordre Toldmaid, just south of the Little Mermaid, stopping at Knippelsbro, Nyhavn, the Opera House, and twice in Holmen along the way.

Single tickets are valid for one hour and cost a fairly steep 36kr, but can also be used on the buses, metro and S-train. Boats sail every 20 minutes until 8pm (7pm on Sundays). A harbour bus also sails from the Opera House to Nyhavn after every performance. See also Canal Tours (p177).

PRACTICALITIES
BUSINESS HOURS

In general, shops in Copenhagen open 9.30 or 10am until 6pm or 7pm from Monday to Friday, and until 3pm or 4pm on Saturday. Most shops are closed on Sundays apart from bakeries and florists. Some local 'kiosks', grocers and branches of Netto supermarket do remain open on Sundays, as do the shops in the Central Station. In a relaxation of the Sunday opening rules, shops are allowed to open for a certain number of Sundays per year, but few take advantage of this. Office hours are typically 9am or 10am to 4pm or 5pm from Monday to Friday.

Note that the Danes tend to eat out early, starting at around 7pm or 7.30pm. Most kitchens close at 10pm and most restaurants expect you to leave by 11.30pm or midnight.

DISCOUNTS

The Copenhagen Card (adult/child aged 10-15 per 24 hour 209/139kr; per 72 hour 439/259kr) gives you free access to around 60 museums in the city and surrounding area as well as free travel on all S-train, metro and bus journeys within the seven travel zones. It has to be said that many of the museums are free or have a free day per week so the value of this is questionable.

ELECTRICITY

Denmark, like most of Europe, runs on 220V (volts), 50Hz (cycles) AC. Check the voltage and cycle (usually 50Hz) used in your home country. Most appliances that are set up for 240V (such as those used in the UK) will handle 220V without modifications and vice versa. It's always preferable to adjust your appliance to the exact voltage if you can – a few items, such as some electric razors and radios, will do this automatically. If your appliance doesn't have a built-in transformer, don't plug a 110/125V appliance (the kind used in the USA and Canada) into a Danish outlet without using a separate transformer.

Denmark uses the 'europlug' with two round pins. Many europlugs and some sockets don't have provision for earth wiring because most local home appliances are double-insulated; when provided, earth usually consists of two contact points along the edge.

If your plugs are of a different design, you'll need an adaptor.

EMERGENCY

Copenhagen is a comparatively safe city, the main risk of crime being from drunkenness or pick pockets – and that is really only late at night and in the main tourist areas. To contact the fire or ambulance services, dial 112, or 114 for police.

The nearest **Central Police Station** (Map p129, D3; ☎ 33 25 14 48) is at Halmtorvet 20, Vesterbro. There is a 24-hour pharmacy, **Steno Apotek** (Map p89, B4; ☎ 33 14 82 66; Vesterbrogade 6, Vesterbro), close to the Central Station. The nearest hospital with an accident and emergency department to the city centre is **Frederiksberg Hospital** (Map p129, B1; ☎ 38 16 38 16; www.frederiksberghospital .dk; Nordre Fasanvej 58, Frederiksberg; 🚌 29 from Rådhuspladsen).

For emergencies:

Ambulance, fire (☎ 112)

Police (☎ 114)

HOLIDAYS

Summer holidays for school children begin around 20 June and end around 10 August. Schools break for a week in mid-October, during the Christmas and New Year period, and for a week, mid-term in late February. Many Danes take their main work holiday during the first three weeks of July.

Banks and most businesses are closed on public holidays, and transport schedules are commonly reduced as well.

Country-wide public holidays include:

New Year's Day (Nytårsdag) 1 January

Maundy Thursday (Skærtorsdag) The Thursday before Easter Day

Good Friday (Langfredag) The Friday before Easter Day

Easter Day (Påskedag) A Sunday in March or April

Easter Monday (2.påskedag) The day after Easter Day

Common Prayer Day (Stor Bededag) The fourth Friday after Easter

Ascension Day (Kristi Himmelfartsdag) The sixth Thursday after Easter

Whitsunday (Pinsedag) The seventh Sunday after Easter

Whitmonday (2.pinsedag) The eighth Monday after Easter

Constitution Day (Grundlovsdag) 5 June

Christmas Eve 24 December (from noon)

Christmas Day (Juledag) 25 December

Boxing Day (2.juledag) 26 December

INTERNET ACCESS

Many cafés and hotels have wireless internet access.

The most central internet café with wireless access is **Boomtown** (Map p89, B3; ☎ 33 32 10 32; www .boomtown.dk; Axeltorv 1-3; per hr Dkr30; 🕑 24hr daily).

LANGUAGE
BASICS

Hello. (polite/ informal)	Goddag/Hej.
Goodbye.	Farvel.
Excuse me/Sorry.	Undskyld.
Yes.	Ja.
No.	Nej.
Thank you.	Tak.
You're welcome.	Selv tak.
Where are you from? (pol/inf)	Hvor kommer De/du fra?

I'm from ...	Jeg er fra ...
Do you speak English?	Taler De engelsk?
I don't understand.	Jeg forstår ikke.

EATING & DRINKING

That was delicious!	Det var lækkert!
I'm a vegetarian.	Jeg er vegetar.
Please bring the bill.	Regningen, tak.
Delicious!	Lækkert!

Local Specialties

Æggekage	Scrambled egg dish with bacon
Flæskesteg	Roast pork, usually with crackling, served with potatoes and cabbage
Frikadeller	Fried minced-pork meatballs, commonly served with boiled potatoes and red cabbage
Gravad laks	Cured or salted salm on marinated in dill and served with a sweet mustard sauce
Stegt flæsk	Crisp-fried pork slices, generally served with potatoes and a parsley sauce

SHOPPING

| How much is it? | Hvor meget koster det? |
| That's too expensive. | Det er for dyrt. |

EMERGENCIES

I'm sick.	Jeg er syg.
Help!	Hjælp!
Call the police.	Ring efter politiet!
Call an ambulance.	Ring efter en ambulance!

DAYS & NUMBERS

today	i dag
tomorrow	i morgen
yesterday	i går

0	nul
1	en
2	to
3	tre
4	fire
5	fem
6	seks
7	syv
8	otte
9	ni
10	ti
11	elve
12	tolv
20	tyve
21	enogtyve
100	hundrede
1000	tusind

MONEY

The Danish krone is usually written DKK in international money markets, Dkr in northern Europe and k within Denmark.

The krone is divided into 100 øre. There are 25-øre, 50-øre, one-krone, two-kroner, five-kroner, 10-kroner and 20-kroner coins. Notes come in 50-, 100-, 200-, 500- and 1000-kroner denominations.

BANKS & ATMS

Banks can be found throughout central Copenhagen. Most are open from 10am to 4pm weekdays (to 6pm on Thursday). Most have ATMs, many of them accessible 24 hours a day and in a multitude of languages. Banks at the airport and Central Station are open longer hours and at weekends.

CHANGING MONEY

The Danske Bank branch at the airport will change currency and give advances on credit cards. If you're on an international ferry to Denmark, you'll typically be able to exchange US dollars and local currencies to Danish kroner on board. The US dollar is generally the handiest foreign currency to bring. However, Danish banks will convert a wide range of other currencies as well, including the euro, Australian dollar, British pound, Canadian dollar, Japanese yen, kroner from Sweden and the Swiss franc. The following branches are convenient and reliable:

Danske Bank Airport (Arrival & Transit Halls; 🕓 6am-10pm)
Forex Central Station (☎ 33 11 22 20; Central Station; 🕓 8am-9pm)

Forex Gothersgade (☎ 33 11 27 00; Gothersgade 8; 🕓 9am-6pm Mon-Fri, 10am-3pm Sat)
Forex Nørreport (☎ 33 32 81 00; Nørre Voldgade 90; 🕓 9am-7pm Mon-Fri, 10am-4pm Sat)

CREDIT CARDS

Credit cards such as Visa and MasterCard (also known as Access or Eurocard) are generally widely accepted in Denmark, although many shops and supermarkets only accept the local bank card Dankort. Charge cards like Amex and Diners Club are also accepted, but not as often.

If a card is lost or stolen, inform the issuing company as soon as possible. Here are Copenhagen numbers for cancelling your cards:
Amex (☎ 70 20 70 97)
Diners Club (☎ 36 73 73 73)
MasterCard, Access, Eurocard (☎ 80 01 60 98)
Visa (☎ 80 01 85 88)

ORGANISED TOURS
CANAL TOURS

You can't visit Copenhagen and *not* take a canal boat trip. Not only is it a fantastic way to see the city, but you see a side of it landlubbers never see. There are two companies that operate guided canal tours during the summer – **DFDS** (☎ 32 96 30 00; www.canaltours .com; embarking points Nyhavn & Gammel

Strand; adult/child 60/25kr; ☼ 10am and every ½-hour until 5pm 24 Mar-22 Jun & 20 Aug-22 Oct, 10am and every ½-hour until 7.30pm 23 Jun-19 Aug; Ⓜ Kongens Nytorv 🚌 15, 19, 26, 1A) and **Netto Boats** (☎ 32 54 41 02; www.havnerundfart.dk; embarking points at Holmens Kirke & Nyhavn; adult/child 30/15kr; ☼ 10am-5pm 2-5 times per hour, 25 Mar-22 Oct; 🚌 6A).

Be aware that, in most boats, you are totally exposed to the elements (which can be quite elemental in Copenhagen harbour, even during the summer). DFDS also runs covered, heated boats in winter. Both companies cover the same routes taking in the main sights including Nyhavn, the Little Mermaid, Holmen, Christianshavn, the harbour and the canal around Slotsholmen. DFDS also offers tours in covered, heated boats during the winter (10.15am and one per hour until 2pm, 23 October to 22 December); tours from the Marriott Hotel (9.45am 24 March to 22 November, 9.55am and every hour until 2.55pm 23 November to 22 December); and three hop-on, hop-off water buses during the summer season (10am to 5pm; see www.canaltours.com for route information and detailed timetable).

WALKING & CYCLING TOURS

Students from the University of Copenhagen offer **Jogging Tours** (☎ 61 60 69 67; www.joggingtours.dk; 70kr)

following two routes – a Royal Tour and a Nørrebro Tour.

Jazz fans can explore the city's rich jazz past with a **Jazz Tour** (☎ 33 45 43 19; www.jazztour.dk; 850kr), which includes a 2- to 3-course dinner with wine and entrance into 2 to 3 clubs, and is run by the Danish Jazz Union.

Copenhagen Walking Tours (☎ 40 81 12 17; www.copenhagen-walkingtours .dk) organises a range of themed tours of the city for, typically, around 100kr per person. **History Tours** (☎ 28 49 44 35; www.historytours.dk; prices vary) leads historically themed walking tours of the city centre, leaving from Højbro Plads. If you don't fancy walking, **City Safari** (☎ 33 23 94 90; www.citysafari.dk) offers cycling tours of the city, departing from the Dansk Arkitectur Center in Christianshavn (see p43). Tours can be adapted to a theme of your choice.

Nightlife Friend (www.nightlifefriend .is) is a tour company with a difference. It started in Reykjavik and has now spread to Copenhagen and Stockholm. For 2,500kr, a local nightlife lover will chaperon you and up to four friends around the city's hotspots for the weekend (9pm to 3am Friday & Saturday), getting VIP entrance to clubs.

Every city has its ghost tour, and Copenhagen is no exception. **Ghost Tours** (☎ 51 92 55 51; www.ghosttour.dk; adult/child 85/60kr) operates a 1½-hour walking tour of the city centre, leaving from Nyhavn at 8pm by advance booking only.

TELEPHONE

The international dialling code for Denmark is +45. Public phones are either coin operated or require a '*telekort*', which you can buy at kiosks and post offices.

TIPPING

Service is included in restaurant bills, and Copenhageners are fairly mean tippers, but you might like to leave 10% if you feel the service has been good.

TOURIST INFORMATION

The **Wonderful Copenhagen Tourist Information Bureau** (Map p89, B3; ☎ 70 22 24 42; www.visitcopenhagen.com; Vester-brogade 4A; 🕑 9am-4pm Mon-Fri, 9am-2pm Sat Jan-Apr, 9am-6pm Mon-Sat May-Jun, 9am-8pm Mon-Sat, 10am-6pm Sun Jul-Aug, 9am-6pm Mon-Sat 1-23 Sept, 9am-4pm Mon-Fri, 9am-2pm Sat, 24 Sep-Dec; S-train Central Station, Vesterport; 🚌 1A, 2A, 5A, 6A) is just across from the main entrance to Tivoli and offers information on the city and Denmark as well as a free hotel booking service.

Use it (Map p106, D5; ☎ 33 73 06 20; www.useit.dk; Rådhusstræde 13; 🕑 11am-4pm Mon-Wed, 11am-6pm Thu, 11am-2pm Fri

15 Sep-14 Jun, 9am-7pm 15 Jun-14 Sep; 🚌 6A) is a young person's information centre that offers help with finding accommodation, what to do in the city and how to meet people.

TRAVELLERS WITH DISABILITIES

Copenhagen tries to be a disabled-friendly city, but facilities do vary greatly and many buildings in the city centre are hindered by the fact that they either have cellar- or raised first-floor entrances which are usually quite narrow and don't allow for ramps. Main major sights and museums are usually well equipped but the older hotels and shops in the city centre are often not accessible. The **Dansk Handicap Forbund** (☎ 39 29 35 55; Kollektivhuset, Hans Knudsens Plads 1A) publishes a free booklet called *København og Frederiksberg… uden besvær?* (Copenhagen & Frederiksberg… without difficulty?) listing hotels, restaurants, museums, churches and entertainment venues that are accessible to travellers with disabilities in the greater Copenhagen area. The booklet is in Danish, but employs international symbols to indicate facilities and can be picked up free at the Copenhagen tourist office.

>INDEX

*ee also separate subindexes for See (p189), Shop (p190), Eat (p191), Drink
)192) and Play (p192).*

000 map pages

⊙ SEE

📷 **SHOP**

000 map pages